The BASIC FINANCIAL FRAMEWORK:

A FINANCIAL TRANSFORMATION JOURNEY

Nana Kwame Akowuah

Revised Edition

Published by Purposed Publishing

www.purposedpublishing.com

Disclaimer

The information contained in this book is provided for educational and informational purposes only. It is not intended as, and should not be construed to be, financial, legal, tax, or investment advice. Readers are encouraged to consult with qualified professionals for advice specific to their individual circumstances. The author and publisher disclaim any liability, loss, or risk incurred as a consequence of the use or application of any content presented herein.

The content presented in this publication reflects the personal interpretations, perspectives, and opinions of the author. It is intended solely for educational and informational purposes. Any references to individuals, organizations, or practices are made respectfully and are not intended to cause harm, defame, or misrepresent any person or entity. The author disclaims any liability for misinterpretation or unintended consequences resulting from the use or application of the material herein.

Biography

Nana Kwame Akowuah is a Ghanaian-born entrepreneur, financial coach, and co-founder / Managing Accountant of Tri-City Business Services. For over a decade, he has coached individuals, families, and small-business owners to build practical money systems budgeting, debt reduction, credit repair, tax readiness, and investing rooted in his Basic Financial Framework.

Nana designs and delivers workshops, multi-week classes, and executive coaching for community groups, churches, nonprofits, and business teams. He has led lectures, seminars, and workshops across the United States and internationally, including trainings for immigrant communities and organizations such as Taptap Send. He has conducted seminars in locations such as Saginaw, Victorious Believers Ministries, First Ward Community Center, and Michigan State University, and he regularly leads faith-based finance courses in Michigan.

Beyond advising, Nana has personally acquired and transformed three businesses in the last two years and continues to mentor new buyers through due diligence, financing, and post-acquisition integration. He holds bachelor's degrees in economics and professional accountancy and an MBA in Finance from Saginaw Valley State University (SVSU).

Nana lives in Michigan with his wife, Ivy Akowuah, and their four daughters. *In The Basic Financial Framework: A Financial Transformation Journey*, he shares the practical playbooks he teaches in coaching rooms and classrooms: simple steps, consistent habits, and faith-driven discipline that create lasting financial change.

Dedication

Dedicated to: Ivy Akowuah

My wife of fourteen years, my confidant, and my constant encouragement.

Thank you for your love that steadied me, your prayers that lifted me, and your patience through late nights of writing and long seasons of building. This book began as my story, but it became our testimony. I love you.

Table of Contents

Acknowledgment

To my wife, **Ivy Akowuah**, for fourteen years, you have been my steady place and my strongest encourager. Thank you for your love, prayers, wisdom, and patience through long nights of writing and the many seasons of building. This book carries your fingerprints on every page.

To my father, **Francis Nana Akowuah**, your integrity, resilience, and counsel shaped my work ethic and my sense of purpose. Thank you for the example you set and the guidance you continue to give.

To my late mother, **Mabel Asmah**, your sacrifices, faith, and courage made room for my dreams. Though you are not here to read these words, your voice and values live within them. This book is part of your legacy.

To my sister, **Dr. Adwoa Boachie**, thank you for your unwavering encouragement, honest feedback, and example of excellence. Your support helped keep me focused and faithful to the vision.

To my mentor, **Dr. Joseph Ofori-Dankwa**, thank you for stretching my thinking, marrying scholarship with practice, and challenging me to lead with purpose. Your belief opened doors and sharpened my path.

Finally, to **all my friends and family who supported and prayed with me** your messages, meals, check-ins, and prayers sustained me more than you know. Thank you for standing with me from the first outline to the final draft.

I am deeply grateful. This book is our shared testimony.

INTRODUCTION

In the pursuit of wealth, the road is often winding, filled with unexpected turns, moments of doubt, and times when faith becomes the only thing that keeps us moving forward. ***The Basic Financial Framework: A Financial Transformation Journey*** is not just a personal story; it's a blueprint for anyone seeking to build a life of financial independence, especially those navigating the complexities of immigration, cultural shifts, and new beginnings.

My name is Nana Kwame Akowuah, and I come from Ghana, a country rich in history, culture, and tradition, but also with its own set of challenges when it comes to creating wealth and opportunity. Like many immigrants, my journey to the United States of America was driven by the hope of a better future not just for me, but for my family and community back home. What I quickly realized was that the pursuit of success in this new land was not merely a matter of hard work. It required faith, faith in God, faith in my own abilities, and faith in the process of growth and learning.

In this book, I will take you on a journey through my experiences, from the decision to leave Ghana to my days as a student, corporate employee, and business owner in America. I will share the pivotal moments that shaped my path, including encounters with inspiring mentors who believed in my potential before I fully saw it in myself.

I will share Practical lessons that anyone whether an immigrant or someone simply striving for financial wholeness can apply to their own life.

As the book reads like a story, I encourage you to read it through to the end. The later chapters become more technical, but staying with the journey will reveal powerful strategic insights and recommendations that can be truly transformative.

You'll learn about the importance of education as the foundation for success, how to save and manage money effectively, and why aligning your financial choices with your deepest values is the key to long-term wealth. I'll show you how to make decisions that build not only wealth, but also preserve your sense of self and purpose, even when the world around you feels uncertain.

This is not a book about overnight success or get-rich-quick schemes. It is a guide for anyone committed to achieving financial wholeness through faith, discipline, and perseverance. Whether you're new to this country, starting over, or simply looking for a roadmap to guide you toward financial independence, you'll find practical strategies, heartfelt advice, and an unwavering belief that with the right mindset, anyone can achieve their goals.

The pursuit of wealth is not just about accumulating money; it's about creating a life of meaning and purpose. My highest hope is that you will find the inspiration, tools, and encouragement to begin or continue your own journey toward financial wholeness.

CHAPTER ONE:
MY ARRIVAL

Lesson: Embracing opportunity for growth with faith in God and faith in yourself.

Makola Market is one of the largest open markets in West Africa.

The humid heat of Ghana hung in the air as I stood in the bustling Makola Market, surrounded by the endless chatter of vendors and the rich aroma of spices. My father had taken me there to prepare for my journey a journey I had dreamed about for years but could hardly believe was now just about to begin.

Among the items we purchased: a winter jacket, something I neither wanted nor thought I'd need. Ghana was warm and familiar; as it turned out, the concept of cold was as foreign to me as the life I was about to step into.

For years, America had existed in my mind as a place of endless opportunity, a land where hard work could transform lives.

Growing up in Kaase, a small town in Kumasi, Ghana, my exposure to the United States was limited to what I saw in movies or heard from those fortunate enough to visit. The images I pieced together created a perfect picture of prosperity people who lived in large houses, drove fancy cars, and seemed to have everything figured out. But my connection to this vision was tenuous. I didn't have immediate family in America, and my mother's siblings, who had moved to the United Kingdom, UK, often spoke of their struggles abroad. Even so, I was determined to carve my own path to get there.

The first glimmer of the possibility of living in the United States came during my time at Kwame Nkrumah University of Science and Technology. I was a first-year student, navigating the chaos of the school's Unity Hall, when I began to notice something students returning from overseas, their suitcases full of phones, gadgets, and stories of success. Most of them had traveled to the United Kingdom, but one friend had gone to the United States. His stories captivated me, and when he introduced me to a travel agency that facilitated student work programs abroad, I knew this was my chance.

This chance came with hurdles. The agency required a passport, application fees, and endless preparation. I took it upon myself to handle it all, keeping my plans secret from my family. It wasn't until I had secured my placement at a Royal Farms gas station in Maryland and scheduled my student visa interview that I told my father. To my surprise, he supported me, even driving me to Accra for the embassy appointment.

The morning of the interview was one I'll never forget. We arrived at the U.S. Embassy at 4:30 a.m., thinking we were early. Instead, we found ourselves at the back of a line that already snaked around the building. By the time the embassy opened, the crowd had tripled, and the nerves I had been suppressing threatened to overwhelm me. The stories I had heard about visa rejections played on a loop in my mind. What if they denied me? What if this dream ended before it even began?

When my turn finally came, I stepped into the interview room, clutching my documents and my faith. The consular officer's questions were direct but kind. She asked about my studies, my plans, and why I wanted to travel to the United States. I spoke honestly about my goals and my position as vice president of the social sciences faculty at my university. To my shock, she barely glanced at my papers. Instead, she smiled, stamped my documents, and told me to return in two days for my visa. I walked out of that room with a profound sense of gratitude and disbelief. Against all odds, I had made it.

A Flight of Faith to a Foreign Land

My flight was booked for January 12, just days after I received my visa. The days leading up to my departure were a blur of preparations and goodbyes. My father's advice stayed with me: "Always have faith and take opportunities when they come." He understood the weight of this moment even more than I did.

On the day of my departure, I boarded a plane for the first time in my life. As the aircraft roared to life and lifted off, I looked out the window at the receding landscape of my home. A mix of fear and excitement settled in my chest. I was leaving behind everything I knew for a chance at something greater, armed with $300, a winter jacket packed in my checked luggage, and a determination that burned brighter than ever.

The journey was smooth until we landed at JFK Airport in New York. The biting cold greeted me the moment I stepped off the plane. It was unlike anything I had ever experienced. I immediately retreated back into the aircraft, where a flight attendant handed me a blanket to shield myself from the frigid wind. Wrapped in that borrowed warmth, I stepped out again, determined to embrace this new world with a brave face.

My courageous approach was tested immediately as it sank in just how solitary my journey would be. There was no family waiting for me at the airport, no familiar faces to guide me. But God has always had a way of placing people in my path.

On the flight, I met a fellow Ghanaian student who recognized me from university. Her brother connected me with a kind stranger a doctor who lived in Manhattan. He offered me a place to stay for the night. To my amazement, the doctor turned out to be the elder brother of one of my closest friends from Ghana. It was a moment that reaffirmed my belief in divine intervention.

As I settled in that night, I reflected on how far I'd come. From the small streets of Kasoa to a Manhattan apartment, and my journey was just starting. The challenges ahead would test me in ways I couldn't yet imagine, but one thing was clear: faith and opportunity had carried me this far, and they would carry me further still.

Welcome to New York

Over the next two days, I navigated New York City with wide-eyed wonder, taking in the towering skyscrapers and the constant hum of activity. My host, Dr. Henry, shared stories about his own journey as an immigrant and offered practical advice for surviving and thriving in America. "It won't be easy," he warned me, "but if you're willing to work hard and trust the process, you'll find your way." His words became a source of comfort, grounding me as I prepared for the next phase of my journey.

When the time came to leave for Maryland, I felt a mix of excitement and apprehension. My first job awaited me at the Royal Farms gas station, but I had no idea what lay ahead. I boarded a bus with a single suitcase and a heart full of hope, determined to make the most of the opportunity I had fought so hard to seize.

As the bus rumbled down the highway, I stared out at the unfamiliar landscape and silently repeated the words my father had told me: "Have faith and take opportunities when they come." It was the mantra that would guide me as I stepped into the unknown.

But within days, I would learn a harsh truth: just getting to America was not enough. The dream of success didn't begin at the airport it began with surviving the unexpected setbacks that would come almost immediately.

A Harsh Welcome to Maryland

When I finally got to Maryland, everything felt confusing as if my entire trip to the U.S. had not been planned at all. I tried reaching Royal Farms on Pulaski Highway, the company I had arranged to work for before leaving Ghana, to confirm my placement since I had come to the U.S. for work. But getting there was a challenge on its own, and when I finally managed to speak with someone, they told me, "We have no placement for you."

My heart sank. My money was running out quickly as I paid for food and stayed in a small motel. I kept in touch with my father, who was trying to find money to send me. I had no clue that I would experience this much chaos but the funny thing was, everything was somehow working out for my good.

Failed Mission

Royal Farms had nothing for me they had no work but I kept going back and talking to the manager. She was really kind and felt genuinely sorry for me. That was the first ram in the bush. She said, "Well, listen, if you're able to find yourself a place to stay around here, I will hire you to work for me."

We had two months left to work, and she was willing to give me a chance. But before I could start, I had to get my Social Security number and a few things in place. The next step was finding a place to stay.

I talked to my dad again, and he started calling his friends anyone he knew who might be able to help.

Dr. Henry, Again

I had to call Dr. Henry the same man who had helped me decide where to go and would have to keep staying in a motel for a while. Dr. Henry knew a few people, and thankfully, he found a friend who also lived in Maryland about six miles from the Royal Farms on Pulaski Highway.

Here's where things became even more interesting. On the third day of staying at the motel, Dr. Henry called me and said, "Listen, I found somebody." That day, the money I had left in my pocket was only fifteen dollars. That was all I had left, which meant I couldn't stay another night at the motel. I was about to be sent out, and I had no idea what I was going to do. But then came the second ram in the bush.

The Kindness of Community

That night, I checked out of the motel, waiting for help. The manager let me sit inside the Royal Farms store to stay warm. I sat near my luggage, watching people come in and out, their lives moving forward while mine felt frozen in place.

At 2:00 a.m., a man I had never met pulled up in a car. "Are you Kwame?" he asked.

“Yes,” I said, standing up.

“Come on. Let’s go.”

His name was Mr. Henry Debrah, and he had driven out of his way, in the middle of the night, just to help a complete stranger.

We didn’t talk much during the drive. When we arrived at his house, he showed me to a small room, pointed to a blanket, and said, “You can sleep here.”

Then he left to go back to work. No questions. No expectations. Just kindness.

For the next few days, I stayed with Mr. Debrah and his family, grateful beyond words. Then, finally, the call I had been waiting for came. The store manager had worked something out with the Social Security office, and I was cleared to start work.

Now, there was only one problem getting there. I had no car, and the gas station was miles away from where I was staying. To make things worse, public transportation was a nightmare to navigate.

Each morning, I had to walk over a mile just to catch the first of two buses that would take me to Pulaski Highway. From the last stop, I had to walk another half mile to the store. And I did this every single day, through the freezing winter air, sometimes trudging through icy sidewalks and biting cold that made each step feel heavier than the last. The work was exhausting, but I was grateful for it. I stocked shelves, cleaned, and helped at the counter. Each hour I worked brought me closer to survival.

By March, I had worked enough to afford a plane ticket back to Ghana, just in time to finish the semester of university that I had left behind.

But returning to school wasn't the victory I expected. I had missed months of assignments. Finals were just a month away, and I was struggling to catch up. My grades suffered. I was too exhausted to focus.

I had thought my three-month work trip to the U.S. would give me a financial boost. Instead, it disrupted my education in ways I hadn't expected.

So, I made a decision.

When the semester ended, I was going back to the United States of America.

This time, I wouldn't just work. I would figure out how to stay, study, and thrive. While I was in Ghana, I called excited again and told them to find me another job. They secured a better-paying position in Delaware Food Giants, paying $11.65 an hour. That was nearly $4 more per hour than Royal Farms had paid me.

The difference was life changing. More pay meant faster savings. More savings meant a real chance at education. Education meant I could stay in the U.S. legally.

When I returned to the U.S. in June, I had a new mindset. I stayed briefly with Mr. Debrah again before moving to Delaware, where I found a host family for $300 a month. This time, I had a better plan.

I told my father, "I am not coming back to Ghana to study. I need to find a way to continue my education in the U.S."

With help from my host family, I researched schools and applied to Saginaw Valley State University (SVSU) in Michigan. They had a good program for international students and were willing to issue an I-20 document, and it was clear that this could be my path to a student visa.

By the end of the summer, I was not just working I was building a real future in the U.S. I was enrolled at SVSU, pursuing a degree in Business Administration in Economics.

I had arrived in America thinking a job would be enough. Now I understood: a job was only the first step. My real life in the U.S. was just beginning.

CHAPTER TWO:
THE RETURN

My wife and I first met as children in Ghana, long before we ever imagined that our futures would be forever intertwined. We attended the same school, and her brother was my classmate. At the time, she was just my friend's younger sister someone I knew but never thought much about beyond our school interactions. Our lives took separate paths, and when her family moved to the United States, we lost touch.

Years later, in 2009, social media brought us back together. Facebook had just started gaining traction, and as I scrolled through my feed one day, I came across her profile. Seeing her again triggered something unexpected I felt drawn to reconnect. I reached out, and we started messaging back and forth, reminiscing about our childhood and catching up on our new lives in different countries. Eventually, I asked for her number, and when I called, we ended up talking for nearly three hours.

It was during that first conversation that I told her, without hesitation, "I'm going to marry you." She laughed, thinking I was joking. At the time, she was in a relationship, and while we remained friends, I never wavered in my belief that she was the one. Over time, as our conversations deepened, we built a strong friendship. She eventually moved back to Ghana to help her mother run a business, and around the same time, she ended her previous relationship.

As we continued to talk, I opened up to her about my struggles in the United States as an international student. Finding work was challenging, and without permanent residency, my opportunities were limited. She offered to help me obtain my green card through marriage. Initially, she saw it as a way to assist me, planning to return to Ghana after the process was complete. But I knew from the beginning that this wasn't just about securing my immigration status I truly wanted to build a life with her.

When she arrived in Saginaw, Michigan, on May 1, 2011, we reunited in person for the first time in years. It felt natural, as if no time had passed. I made it clear that I wasn't interested in a marriage of convenience I wanted something real. After some thought, she agreed, and on July 18, 2011, we got married.

'Til Debt Do Us Part

Marriage was beautiful, but it also came with its share of challenges. Adjusting to life together in a new country, away from family and familiarity, tested us in ways we hadn't expected. At the same time, I was facing a major career roadblock. I had my degree, but without internship experience, I struggled to secure a job.

Bills were piling up, and the pressure of providing for my new family weighed heavily on me. It was at this moment that I learned one of my first major financial lessons: when faced with a roadblock, don't just look for an escape look for a solution. For me, that solution was further education.

In January 2012, I enrolled in a master's program in finance at Saginaw Valley State University. I took on an intense course load, determined to complete the program in just one year. I pushed myself harder than I ever had before, knowing that every class, every assignment, and every sleepless night was a step toward a stable future. When I graduated in 2013, our lives were once again about to change my wife was pregnant with our first daughter.

That same year, I also attempted my first business venture an entertainment center in Ghana. I had saved up money, bought gaming consoles, televisions, and computers, and partnered with my mentor, Dr. Joseph Ofori-Dankwa, and other investors to launch the business.

I believed in the idea, but the biggest lesson I learned was that businesses require constant presence and attention. Since I had to return to the United States, the business struggled in my absence and eventually collapsed within a month. This experience taught me that investing in a business without being physically present or ensuring strong management was a risk I couldn't afford to take again.

The journey of love, marriage, and building a future together had truly begun, and with it came lessons that would shape our financial and personal lives for years to come.

Even with my master's degree, I quickly realized that my current education alone wasn't enough. I was stuck in a cycle overqualified for entry-level positions but lacking the experience needed for higher roles. Every rejection letter was a reminder that education, while valuable, is only one part of the equation. I needed to gain practical skills that employers would find indispensable.

At one point, my wife and I faced an incredibly difficult financial period. Bills were stacking up, our savings were depleting, and despite my qualifications, I couldn't find steady work. This was a turning point in my understanding of financial literacy. One of the biggest lessons I learned was the importance of adaptability. No matter how much you prepare, life will throw challenges your way, and your ability to pivot will determine your success.

In 2015, while struggling to find stability, I made an important trip to Ghana. While it was meant to be a short visit, it became the last time I would see my mother. We spent time together, shared stories, and I cherished every moment, not knowing that just a few months later, she would pass away. That loss shook me to my core, reinforcing the lesson that life is unpredictable. It also taught me the importance of having financial preparedness not just for business and investments, but also for family emergencies and unexpected events.

During this period, I met a friend who was a CPA. He explained that accounting was a field with high demand and a clearer pathway for immigrants like me. I realized that shifting my focus to accounting could open doors that finance alone hadn't. I consulted with my mentor, Dr. Dankwa, and professors, mapped out a plan, and in January 2015, I enrolled in a 45-credit program for another Bachelor of Professional Accountancy.

The year was unbelievably challenging. My wife had just given birth to our second daughter, Victoria, and we were struggling financially. Our cars were repossessed, rent was becoming an issue, I lost my mom, and I had to make every dollar stretch. Despite the hardship, I held onto my faith.

John 14 became my daily scripture: *"Do not let your hearts be troubled. You believe in God; believe also in me."*

I started my pursuit of professional accounting education with a diverse group of students working toward the same goal. We pushed each other, studied together, and stayed accountable. By the end of the year, I secured a full-time job at Plante Moran as an auditor and started working in January of 2016. This opportunity changed the trajectory of my life.

For the first time, I had financial stability. My salary allowed us to pay off debts, build savings, and start thinking long-term. But I also knew that a corporate job wasn't my final destination. My entrepreneurial spirit had always been strong, and in 2017, I officially started my own accounting firm, Globadigm Consulting.

The road to this point had been long, filled with setbacks and lessons, but every struggle prepared me for the moment when I could finally say: I built this firm. It was a new beginning that opened the door to much more!

CHAPTER THREE: FROM CLARITY TO ACTION

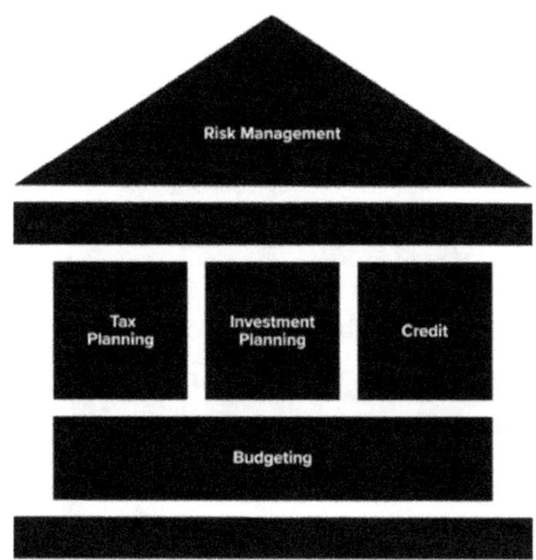

The financial distress I faced after arriving in the United States. forced me to confront my money habits.

As I recounted earlier, it did not take me long before I realized something had to change. The turning point was a deep dive into personal finance, out of which I developed what I call the Basic Financial Framework: A holistic approach to managing money with purpose, precision, and discipline.

Before diving into tactics like budgeting, credit repair, or investing, it's critical to prepare your most important economically, your mindset. This chapter lays out four foundational principles that are key to the effectiveness of the Basic Financial Framework system.

Without these, any financial strategy or budget will struggle to take root for your long-term benefit. These principles are:

1) Avoid ambiguity by being specific.
2) Learn the right information.
3) Understand that information and how it applies to your situation.
4) Apply consistently what you learn.

Let's unpack each in detail.

1. Avoid Ambiguity

One of the biggest obstacles to financial clarity is ambiguity. People often describe their finances in vague terms: "I have too much debt," or "I don't make enough money," or "I have too many bills."

While these feelings are real, they're not actionable because finance is about numbers, not feelings.

Vague statements create a fog of anxiety without pointing to a solution. In fact, ambiguity often leads to avoidance. Studies show 22% of consumers even avoid checking their finances altogether (with rates even higher among younger adults).

Many only peek at fragments like account balances and ignore the full picture of their financial health. This avoidance is an emotional response to feeling overwhelmed or afraid of facing the truth.

Ironically, staying in the dark increases anxiety and stress. The antidote is specificity. If you can quantify a problem, you can start solving it.

Replace "too much debt" with exact numbers: e.g., "I owe $47,000 in student loans and $6,000 on credit cards." Instead of "I don't make enough," say "I bring in $4,000 a month, but my expenses total $5,200." Here's an example:

I had a friend come to me for financial help. Sitting across from me, she was sobbing, "I'm drowning in debt."

Here is what we did to solve the problem:

We sat down and listed every debt: it turned out to be four debts totaling under $6,000. Writing down all her obligations transformed an overwhelming, ambiguous fear into a concrete target. In just six weeks, with clarity and focus, she wiped out that debt entirely. This illustrates a powerful truth: **ambiguity creates anxiety, but specificity creates strategy.**

Mental health research backs this up: keeping finances vague in your head can magnify worry, whereas writing down all your debts and bills provides clarity and actually reduces the emotional weight of the debt.

It's a form of relief: by putting the exact numbers on paper, you take away the mystique surrounding your debt and make it a finite problem. In turn, this frees up mental energy to formulate solutions. Psychologists refer to this as "offloading" worries: Listing your financial concerns explicitly can reduce their mental grip and give you back bandwidth for solving the problem.

Simply put, you can't fix what you haven't clearly defined. Count it, measure it, list it, because if you can count it, you can solve it.

2. Learn the Right Financial Information

The second key to leveraging the Basic Financial Framework system is getting the right information. In the age of TikTok and Facebook advice, misinformation or half-truths abound. Managing your money is hard enough without conflicting and often wrong information floating around on social media. Buying into these common myths, especially, can be harmful, leading you astray and undermining your financial health.

In other words, bad information can trap you; good information can free you.

Consider this simple illustration:

I once asked a group of people, "Would you jump out of a plane for $1 million?"

Everyone said no. Then I added, "The plane is on the ground." Suddenly, everyone's answer changed. One crucial piece of information completely altered the decision. The same goes for money. If you only hear sound bites or myths without context, you can make the wrong choices.

Another example: I often meet people who say, "I registered my business to save on taxes." When I probe further, they sometimes believe that having an LLC means they can write off personal expenses (Like cars or luxury purchases tax-free). That's simply not true. Tax experts consistently debunk this misconception. Forming an LLC by itself does not confer special tax breaks.

The IRS doesn't even recognize an "LLC" as a tax class, so your income is generally taxed the same way as before unless you deliberately change your tax election.

In fact, thinking that you can deduct personal lifestyle expenses just by owning a business is "flat out false." As one financial planner put it, setting up an LLC does not magically make your cars or Rolexes tax deductions.

Unfortunately, such bad advice spreads easily online, and many people follow it without understanding the consequences. Pursue accurate, relevant information for your situation. That means double-checking what you hear and getting advice from reputable sources (or professionals) who understand things like your income level, tax bracket, business model, and goals.

Don't rely on a one-size-fits-all tip from an X thread or a viral video. The cost of wrong information can be huge:

From missed opportunities to legal troubles or financial loss. By contrast, the right information, tailored to you, empowers you to make sound decisions. Remember, one key detail can change everything. So, before you act on any financial tip, make sure you've got all the facts straight.

3. Understand the Information

Having the right facts and figures is only part of the equation. You also have to truly understand the information you receive and how it applies to you. Financial strategies are not one size-fits-all.

A tactic that works wonders for someone else might backfire or fizzle for you if misapplied. Misunderstanding good information can be just as dangerous as having bad information.

Take debt, for example. Some gurus proclaim, "all debt is bad, always avoid it." It's easy to internalize that as gospel without deeper thought. As financial expert Martin Lewis famously said, "Debt is like fire. It is a powerful tool if used right, but use it wrong and you will get burned."

In practical terms, not all debt is created equal. A reasonable mortgage or a student loan investing in your future can be "good debt" when managed well, whereas high-interest credit card balances are clearly "bad debt."

Yet, I've met people who, misunderstanding the nuance, refuse to ever take a low-interest loan even when it could improve their situation (Say, to refinance expensive debt or invest in a profitable education), and conversely, people who take on risky debt thinking it's automatically a smart move. Understanding context is critical. A recent interview with a personal finance expert pointed out that

There's a widespread lack of understanding about nuances like which debts are harmful versus which might not be so bad. Make sure you determine what is right for you!

Blindly following a rule ("Never have debt" or "Always leverage debt") without understanding why can lead you astray.

The same goes for business or tax advice: You might hear, "Set up an LLC to save on taxes", a tip that has a kernel of truth for certain cases (For instance, high-earning self-employed folks might save on self-employment tax by electing S-Corp status under an LLC).

If you don't understand the mechanics, you might think just having an LLC is a ticket to write off personal expenses (Which, as discussed, it isn't).

Nuance matters: Know for whom and under what conditions a strategy applies. If a piece of advice mentions a benefit, dig into the how.

Ask: Does this apply to someone with my income or my goals? What are the potential downsides or requirements? In the Basic Financial Framework, we emphasize sound comprehension over blind belief. It's not enough to parrot financial tips.

You need to grasp their meaning. This might involve some extra homework (like reading reputable articles or consulting a professional) to truly see how a concept works. This effort pays off by preventing costly misunderstandings. In short, never execute a strategy you don't fully understand. With understanding, you can adapt general financial knowledge into a personalized plan that actually works for you.

4. Apply the Information

Finally, once you've eliminated ambiguity, gathered the right information, and understood it, you must act on it. Knowledge without action is useless. You can have precise numbers, a head full of great advice, and a clear understanding of finance...but if you fail to execute, nothing in your life will change. It's like having a map and a car full of gas, but never driving to your destination.

While this principle of application sounds obvious, many people stumble trying to enact it. How often do we know what we should do, but procrastinate or do the opposite?

For instance, millions of Americans budget on paper but don't stick to it in practice. A 2023 survey found that 83% of United States of Americans admit to overspending, and even among those who have a monthly budget, 84% still exceed their budget at times.

In other words, having a plan isn't the hard part; following it consistently is.

The best debt payoff strategy won't help if you never make the extra payments.

A meticulously crafted budget is pointless if you don't actually restrain your spending according to it.

You might understand the ins and outs of investing, but that knowledge alone won't grow your wealth unless you put money into the market. To drive home this point, I often invoke a popular saying: "Knowledge without application is useless."

Martial artist Bruce Lee put it bluntly: "Knowing is not enough, we must do."

In teaching personal finance to students, educators stress that reading and learning must translate into tangible steps. For example, actually opening an account, actually setting aside the $25 a week, actually cutting up the extra credit card.

Information becomes transformed only through implementation.

In the Basic Financial Framework system, every piece of advice comes with an action plan. If we calculate your true income vs. expenses, we'll then adjust your spending or increase your income. If we create a debt payoff plan, you'll start making the payments according to the schedule, immediately. If we determine an investment strategy, you'll set up automatic contributions (even if small at first) so it can be put into practice.

There is zero room for complacency where you nod your head but do nothing. Don't let "analysis paralysis" or the comfort of planning stall you.

Execution is everything. The habits and discipline you build by acting on what you know are what produce results. And remember, action doesn't have to be perfect. It's better to start imperfectly (and learn along the way) than to never start at all. Over time, those actions become habits, and those habits yield financial stability and growth.

Recap and Next Steps

Let's recap the foundational pillars of the Basic Financial Framework:

1. **Avoid Ambiguity and be specific:** Confront your finances with concrete numbers. Stop the "around-ish" talk; know exactly what you owe, earn, and spend.

   Specificity brings clarity and turns anxiety into a solvable puzzle.

   If you can measure it, you can manage it.

2. **Get the Right Information:** Seek advice grounded in facts and relevant to your situation. Don't fall for viral myths or one-size-fits-all tips. Bad information wastes time or money, whereas solid information (from credible sources or professionals) gives you an edge.

3. **Understand the Information:** Contextualize financial knowledge. Dig deeper into the "why" and "how" before you leap. Recognize that what's smart for someone else might not be for you, and vice versa. Nuance matters: whether it's distinguishing good debt from bad or understanding the fine print of a tax strategy.

4. **Apply the Information:** All the knowledge in the world means nothing if you don't implement it. Turn plans into action. Consistency and execution are the secret sauce behind every success story. Even small steps, done regularly, beat grand plans never put into practice.

   As the saying goes, you have to work the plan for the plan to work.

These four principles are the building blocks of the Basic Financial Framework system. By adopting them, you prepare your mind and habits to make the most of any financial strategy.

With this foundation in place, we can now move from mindset to method. In the next chapter, we'll begin

Constructing your Basic Financial Framework system step by step, starting with the budgeting framework that truly changed my life. With clarity and the right approach, you'll be ready to take action and transform your financial future.

Let's begin!

CHAPTER FOUR: BASIC FINANCIAL FRAMEWORK - BUDGETING SYSTEM

One of the first major realizations I had was this: you cannot have a successful personal finance plan without a robust and functional budgeting system. When I first started taking personal finance seriously, I turned to books and programs like those from Dave Ramsey and other thought leaders.

They all echoed the same message: Budgeting is essential, but understanding its importance and actually doing it are two different things.

I have to be honest. I struggled with budgeting, so if you feel the same way, you are not alone! I created dozens of spreadsheets, tried app after app, and spent countless nights tracking my income and expenses, only to fall short.

I overspent, missed bills, and often left out recurring expenses. It was discouraging. Even with an emergency fund in place, I struggled to follow a consistent budget.

The turning point came during a long conversation with my wife. I had initially thought budgeting success depended on her participation, but I soon realized budgeting was something I had to own myself.

Over time, as I mentored friends and family, I noticed a pattern: Almost everyone hits a wall when it comes to budgeting. It was a shared struggle.

We all know budgeting matters, but many of us fail to stick to it. That's when I developed the strategy that became the foundation of what I now call the Basic Financial Framework Budgeting System. It's a five-step process that has helped many people, myself included, create a budget that is not only functional but also sustainable.

Mastering Money Starts With Finance Fundamentals

Step 1: Set a Clear, Meaningful Goal

One of the first mistakes I made was budgeting without a goal. In essence, I budgeted because I was told to, not because I had a compelling reason to take control of my money.

Now I know that successful budgeting starts with a strong why.

Without a goal, your budget will become an empty exercise. Your goal can be short-term (For example, saving $2,000 for a car repair) or long-term (Like the goal of buying a home). In my case, I tied my budget to paying off debt and building an emergency fund so I could eventually purchase my first home.

Once I had that specific goal, I became naturally more consistent in my budget practice. The motivation came from knowing exactly what I was working toward. Budgeting for the sake of budgeting rarely works. Budgeting toward a vision, however, is powerful. Once you reach one goal, set another. Keep moving forward by letting your goals drive your budgeting discipline and desire.

Step 2: Review Your Finances Thoroughly

Next, I performed a full review of my financial history. I printed the past three months of statements from every bank account and credit card I had. This step revealed my true spending patterns I didn't want to rely on assumptions; I needed data. Why three months? It gives a clearer picture than a shorter-term analysis of your financials.

Consider that some bills only appear quarterly, so looking at just one month means that you could miss important expenses. In some cases, you may need six months of data, but three months is a great starting point. From this information, I identified my recurring expenses, my spontaneous purchases, and discovered some spending patterns that surprised me.

After reviewing three months of my transactions, I realized I needed a clearer framework to see where my money was going and why.

I developed a four-part categorization system that became the backbone of my budgeting method. Instead of grouping expenses arbitrarily (or just by merchant or product type), I organized them by **necessity** and **predictability**. This way, each dollar I spent was identified as something I either **needed** or **wanted**, and as either **fixed** (predictable) or **variable** (fluctuating).

Bucketing your finances into clear categories helps track funds for each purpose.

For example, an illustration of colorful buckets overflowing with coins can symbolize distinct savings or spending categories. By assigning every expense to a bucket whether it's a necessity or a discretionary treat you gain a visual sense of how each dollar is allocated. This clarity is crucial for intentionally managing your cash flow.

We can categorize spending into the following **four main segments**, designed to help you manage your cash flow more intentionally:

Necessary \ Fixed Expenses

These are essential, recurring payments that generally remain consistent from month to month. They are tied to obligations, well-being, or long-term goals. Examples include:

Tithes: a spiritual or personal commitment.

Debt Payments: e.g., car loans, student loans.

Investments: automatic contributions to retirement or brokerage accounts.

Rent or Mortgage: housing costs.

Gym Membership: e.g., a Planet Fitness membership for physical wellness.

Internet & Phone Services: utility-like bills for connectivity.

Family Support: regular financial support sent to loved ones.

Licenses and Professional Fees: recurring fees for maintaining licenses or services.

Life Insurance: insurance premiums for life coverage.

Because these expenses are both **necessary and fixed**, they should be automated and paid from a dedicated "bills" account to ensure they are never missed.

Automating these predictable obligations is a classic "set and forget" strategy that prevents late fees and stress. In practice, some people maintain a separate checking account solely for fixed essentials (like rent, loans, insurance).

You can have part of your paycheck directly deposited into this bill's account and set all these payments to autopay. This way, your must-pay expenses are always covered first, on time, and with minimal effort.

Necessary Variable Expenses

These are expenses essential to daily living, but the amounts fluctuate month to month. You can't eliminate these costs, but you **can** prepare for them by tracking averages and setting spending limits. Examples include:

Utilities: electricity, gas, and water bills that change with usage.

Home & Personal Care: cleaning supplies, toiletries, hygiene products.

Groceries: food and household grocery items.

School-Related Costs: fees, supplies, kids' lunches, and activities.

To manage this category, consider using a **single credit card with a manageable limit** dedicated to these variable necessities.

Charge only these essentials to the card, and automate as many of them as possible (For example, set utility bills to auto-charge the card). Crucially, **pay off this card in full each month** to avoid interest. Using a credit card in this way has two benefits: it simplifies tracking (all variable needs appear on one statement) and it can earn you rewards on things you have to buy anyway.

For instance, some cards offer cash back for groceries or utilities, effectively giving a small discount on your necessary spending. By keeping the credit limit low, you also naturally cap how much can be spent in this category, which helps prevent overspending.

Remember, the key is discipline: treat the card like a debit account. If you don't have the cash to pay for a purchase immediately, don't put it on the card. Used wisely, this strategy can build credit and even yield perks, without costing you extra.

Discretionary Fixed Expenses

These are **non-essential** but **consistent** monthly costs. Think of them as the wants that come in the form of subscriptions or memberships. They enhance your life but aren't strictly necessary. Examples include:

Apple Music: or any music streaming subscription.

Netflix: or other video streaming services.

Amazon Prime or other Subscriptions: monthly membership fees or regular subscription boxes.

Since these are optional expenses, it's important to prevent them from intruding on money meant for necessities. A handy tactic is to assign all such discretionary subscriptions to a **prepaid debit card** or a checking account with no overdraft (and keep a limited balance in it). Load this card/account with the total amount you budget for fun subscriptions each month. If you decide to cancel a service, simply stop funding the prepaid card and let the subscription lapse. This approach spares you the hassle of contacting each provider to cancel; the charges will just fail once funds dry up. It also ensures that if money is tight, your non-essentials automatically pause rather than siphon funds from essential bills. In fact, some savvy budgeters suggest using reloadable prepaid cards for subscriptions specifically so "if I want the subscription to continue, I toss some money on the card; if not, the company can keep trying to charge a card with no money". By walling off "fun but optional" expenses in their own silo, you guarantee they never interfere with more important financial obligations.

Discretionary Variable Expenses

This final category covers the expenses that are **neither necessary nor predictable.** They vary each month based on your lifestyle, habits, or one-time whims. In other words, these are your true "wants" and impulse spends. Examples include:

Shopping: non-essential retail purchases (clothes, gadgets, etc.).

Coffee & Snacks: those café runs and vending machine treats.

Dining Out: restaurant meals, takeout, bar tabs.

Entertainment: movies, concerts, events, hobbies.

Beauty Services: salons, spa treatments, cosmetic products.

I recommend managing this category with **cash (or a cash-equivalent envelope system)**. Decide on a monthly allowance for your discretionary-variable spending, an amount you're willing to spend on "fun" that month, and withdraw exactly that amount in cash. Once that cash is gone, it's gone.

Using cash creates a natural stopping point that card spending doesn't: when your wallet is empty, you simply cannot spend further in this category until next month. This approach establishes a hard boundary that curbs impulse buying.

Behavioral research shows that parting with physical cash makes you more mindful of spending, as it feels more tangible than swiping a card. In fact, the classic envelope budgeting method leverages this psychology: watching the cash in an envelope dwindle is a built-in signal to slow down spending.

By living on a cash budget for non-essentials, you'll find yourself thinking twice about that spontaneous purchase or daily latte. It's a simple trick to impose discipline on the most capricious part of your budget.

ESSENTIAL - FIXED	ESSENTIAL - VARIABLE
Health Insurance, Rent/Mortgage	Groceries Utilities Gas

DISCRETIONARY - FIXED	DISCRETIONARY - VARIABLE
Gym Membership TV Subscriptions	Dining Out Entertainment Shopping

NOTES

Implementation Plan

Facing the Hard Realities

There were seasons when we couldn't pay everything. Some debts like two auto loans and a credit card had to remain unpaid temporarily. Our credit scores plummeted into the low 500s, and we couldn't even qualify to move to a new apartment. It was humbling and painful, but it was also necessary.

If we had continued trying to pay everyone with money we didn't have, we would have sacrificed our family's stability. Instead, we chose to focus on what we could control and rebuild from there.

Negotiating and Rebuilding

Two years later, once our finances stabilized, I revisited the debts that had gone into collections. I walked into the credit union and explained my situation honestly. To my surprise, they were willing to work with me. They couldn't remove the debt from collections immediately, but they agreed to reduce the balance as I made consistent payments.

That conversation marked a turning point. Over the next two years, I paid it off in full. As our debts reduced, our credit slowly began to recover. With consistency and transparency, our financial foundation grew stronger.

Balancing Debt and Growth

One area where I slightly diverged from Dave Ramsey's philosophy was in my belief that paying off debt alone isn't enough. If your income remains low, you can't achieve financial freedom no matter how debt-free you are.

So, while we dedicated a set portion of our income to debt repayment, we also invested in education and skill development to increase our earning potential. That decision became one of the most important financial choices we ever made.

As our income grew, we increased our monthly debt payments but we also began setting aside small amounts for savings and investments. Even modest contributions helped us build momentum toward financial independence.

The Outcome

Our journey wasn't quick or easy. It took years of budgeting, sacrifice, and discipline. But slowly, our financial suffocation turned into breathing room. Our debts decreased, our credit improved, and our mindset about money completely changed.

Debt management, for us, was more than a process it was a path to reclaiming control over our lives. And by mastering that, we built the foundation for everything else that followed.

Debt Management: Regaining Control through the Snowball Method

When my wife and I finally sat down to face our financial challenges head-on, the first major issue we had to tackle was debt management. Much of the financial pressure we felt came from being surrounded by debt credit cards, personal loans, auto loans, and student loans. The weight of it all created what I called financial suffocation. We knew that if we didn't take control, our financial future would slip further out of reach.

Through the Dave Ramsey program, I learned key principles about debt management that I still use today. I came to understand that managing debt isn't just about numbers it's about courage, discipline, and having a system that helps you regain control of your financial life.

Choosing a Strategy: Avalanche vs. Snowball

Our first decision was to choose a method for paying off our debts. We considered the Avalanche Method, which targets the highest-interest debt first. The logic is simple: interest is the true cost of debt, so paying off the most expensive debt saves money in the long run.

However, our highest-interest debt was also our largest including a student loan at over 15% interest. With our limited income, those balances felt impossible to attack quickly. We needed momentum, not just logic.

That's when we turned to the Snowball Method, a system promoted by Dave Ramsey that focuses on paying off the smallest debts first. Each victory no matter how small built motivation and restored confidence.

Building a Debt Budget

We created a specific monthly amount dedicated solely to debt repayment. This amount became part of our budget and never changed, even when times were hard. Every month, we paid the minimums on all debts and directed any extra money toward the smallest balance.

Once one debt was paid off, we rolled that same payment amount into the next smallest debt like a snowball gaining speed downhill. This method gave us a clear system to follow and, more importantly, a sense of progress.

We also made a crucial rule: once a credit card was paid off, we stopped using it completely. This discipline helped us avoid slipping back into old habits.

In practice, implementing this structure often involves leveraging multiple bank accounts or tools. For example, the image above shows a person budgeting with several accounts on a laptop, highlighting how dividing money into separate accounts or "buckets" can simplify management.

By setting clear boundaries for each category, you ensure essentials are covered automatically while keeping discretionary spending in check. The strategies below outline how to put the four-segment system into action.

To make this four-part budgeting system practical and sustainable, I adopted a few core strategies and am passing them along to you!

These will help automate your finances and maintain the discipline needed for each category:

Automate All Fixed and Necessary Payments: Set up a dedicated checking account (or sub-account) exclusively for your **Necessary Fixed** expenses, such as rent, loan payments, tithes, and so on.

Have a portion of your income directly deposited into this account sufficient to cover all those bills. Then automate every recurring bill to be paid from that account (Using your bank's bill pay or auto-debit from the provider).

This way, your must-pay expenses are handled without manual effort each month. Separating these bills from your spending money also ensures you **never accidentally dip into funds needed for essentials.**

Automation further guarantees you won't miss payments or incur late fees. In short, you've firewalled your fixed obligations so they're always covered first a huge stress reducer.

Use a Credit Card for Variable Necessities: As mentioned, assign one low-limit credit card solely for your **Necessary**

Variable expenses (groceries, gas, utilities, etc.). Treat this card like a charge card: put your variable necessities on it, but **do not use it for anything else.**

Importantly, pay off the entire balance every month.

This approach consolidates all your fluctuating essential spending in one place for easy tracking. It can also work in your favor through rewards points or cash back on routine expenses, effectively giving you a small rebate on your needs.

Keep the credit limit modest (in line with your typical monthly needs budget) to prevent overspending beyond your means. Using a card also builds your credit history, **provided you pay on time and in full.**

To avoid any temptation or confusion, you might even nickname the card in your online banking (e.g., "Groceries & Bills Card") and set up auto-pay so you never miss the due date.

Create Specialized Savings Buckets: To tackle larger goals and non-monthly expenses, create separate **savings accounts** earmarked for each purpose. For example, you might have a "Child Care" fund, a "Home Down Payment" fund, an "Annual Insurance Premiums" fund, etc. Automate contributions to these accounts based on your pay schedule; even a small automatic transfer each week or month will steadily grow these funds. Using multiple savings buckets(often called sinking funds) makes it easy to **see your progress toward each goal** at a glance.

For instance, you could maintain an emergency fund, a holiday gift fund, and a vacation fund separately; when you view your accounts, you can immediately tell how close you are to each target.

This not only keeps you organized but also psychologically motivates you, as each account feels like a "bucket" filling up with purpose. Plus, by segregating money for big upcoming expenses, you won't be caught off guard when those bills come due the money's already there waiting.

Use Budgeting Tools: Take advantage of modern budgeting apps and tools to track and visualize your spending in real time. Apps like Mint, You Need A Budget (YNAB), PocketGuard, or even a simple spreadsheet can sync with your accounts and help categorize transactions. In fact, basic budgeting apps will connect to your financial accounts, **track your spending, and categorize expenses so you can see where your money is going.**

Many apps allow you to set alerts or limits on category spending, for example, warning you when you're nearing your monthly dining-out budget. They also provide helpful visuals (pie charts, trend graphs) to quickly show if your spending aligns with your plan. If apps aren't your style, a well-designed spreadsheet or a manual ledger can work too; the key is to review it regularly (see next point).

The goal of any tool is to give you clarity and accountability. Choose one that fits your personality. If you love detail and control, YNAB or a spreadsheet might be ideal; if you prefer set-and-forget simplicity, an automated app like Mint could suit you. Using tools takes the guesswork out of budgeting and lets you immediately spot problem areas or opportunities to save.

Monthly Financial Check-Ins: At the end of each month, set aside a brief time to review your finances. Think of it as a **monthly money date** with yourself.

During this check-in, go over each category:

- Did you stay within your budget for discretionary spending?
- Do you have any new necessary expenses cropped up?
- Are you closer to your savings goals?

Update your budget spreadsheet or app with the month's final numbers, and adjust your category allocations for the next month if needed. Regular monthly reviews create a feedback loop; they impose accountability and let you course-correct quickly. In fact, doing routine check-ins ensures you **stay on track and can make necessary adjustments promptly** rather than letting small issues snowball.

Use this time to also celebrate wins (Came in under budget on groceries? paid off a debt? Fantastic! Cheer yourself on but don't splurge to reward yourself!) and set intentions for the next month.

These meetings don't have to be long or complicated; even 15-30 minutes is enough to realign your money with your goals. Over time, you'll find that these small habits keep you in control and aware of your financial trajectory, which is exactly the point of having a structured budget in the first place.

By categorizing your spending into these four strategic segments and following the implementation steps above, you create a **balanced, intentional cash flow plan.**

Essentials are protected and automated, goals are steadily funded, and "fun" spending is kept within healthy limits. This system brings order to your finances and puts **you** in charge of where each dollar goes, instead of wondering where it went.

With a bit of upfront effort to set up accounts and automate, your budget largely runs on autopilot and you just steer it with those regular check-ins.

The result is a budgeting method that is **practical, sustainable, and highly effective** in helping you align your money with your priorities.

Enjoy the peace of mind that comes with knowing your financial bases are covered and that you're actively working toward your goals, one segment at a time!

CHAPTER FIVE: INVESTMENT

Investment is a Wealth-Building Tool (Only After a Solid Foundation is Built.)

When people hear the word "wealth," they often immediately think of investing stocks, real estate, crypto, and all the glamorous headlines. It's true that investing is a powerful driver of wealth, but it might surprise you that it shouldn't be your first step.

I didn't begin my financial journey with stocks or real estate; I started with basics like budgeting and credit management. The reason is simple: without a strong financial foundation (emergency savings, controlled debt, good credit, etc.), investing can turn into a risky gamble instead of a wealth-building tool.

In fact, personal finance experts commonly advise securing an emergency fund and paying down high-interest debt before diving into investments. Skipping those steps is a recipe for stress or worse, needing to pull out investments at a loss when an emergency hits.

Investment should come only after you've gotten your financial house in order. With that foundation in place, you're ready to make your money start working for you.

What is Investing? (as a verb)

At its core, **investing means creating a system where your money earns more money for you.** Instead of trading your time directly for dollars, you put existing dollars to work to generate additional income or growth. The stock market is one of the most popular ways to do this.

For example, when you buy shares of companies like Apple or Google, you're essentially handing your money to those businesses' highly skilled teams and saying: "Grow my money as your business grows."

If the company grows and its value rises, the value of your share increases; your money **grows** along with the company's success. Some companies even pay you part of their profits (called **dividends**) just for being a shareholder, providing you with cash payouts on top of any price appreciation.

Even small amounts of money can grow into substantial wealth given enough time and the right rate of return. The figurines on the coin stacks above illustrate how one individual's modest savings (left) can multiply into a far larger sum (right) when continuously invested and compounded over many years.

For example, the U.S. stock market (S&P 500 index) has historically returned around 10% per year on average. At that rate, an investment will roughly double in value every seven years (per the "Rule of 72"). Over decades, this compounding effect is dramatic.

Money invested earns profits, those profits get reinvested to earn even more, and so on. This is essentially "your money-making money."

By contrast, cash that's not invested (or low-yield savings) barely grows and loses purchasing power over time due to inflation.

Investing is how you put financial growth on autopilot.

While stocks are a common route, **investment is much broader than the stock market**. You can invest in real estate (where your property can appreciate or generate rental income), bonds (lending money in exchange for interest), or even in your own or others' businesses.

The key is that **investing should be personal and intentional**. It's not about chasing someone else's hot tip or the hype of the moment; it's about choosing a strategy that fits your goals and life situation. Many people lose money not because "investing doesn't work," but because they jumped in without the right strategy or stage of readiness.

For example, frequent trading or speculative bets without proper knowledge often backfire. Studies show that **over 97% of day traders end up losing money** in the long run. The lesson is that investing isn't actually that complicated, but it must be done with discipline and purpose.

Once you have a solid financial base and a clear plan, investing becomes the exciting part of your financial journey where your dollars start to do the heavy lifting for you.

Before we dive into specific investment options, I want to share a model that helped me (and many others) think about investing in a structured way. I call it **The Five Levels of Investment.**

Whether you're currently broke or already wealthy, you're always at some level in this framework. These five levels build on each other like rungs of a ladder; if you skip one, your whole investment strategy can become unstable.

So, let's walk through them one by one.

The Five Levels of Investment

Level 1: Invest in Yourself

This first level is the most overlooked, yet the most crucial: *You, Inc.* Before expecting your money to earn more money, you need to invest in **building your own skills, mindset, and earning potential.** Your best investment is still **you**. Improving yourself increases your capacity to generate income and make wise financial decisions, which in turn provides more money to invest later.

Legendary investor, Warren Buffett, stresses this point: "Generally speaking, investing in yourself is the best thing you can do… If you've maximized your talent, you've got a tremendous asset that can return tenfold." In practical terms, Level 1 means devoting time and sometimes money to personal growth. For example, consider:

Education and Skills: Learn a new skill that can increase your income. This could be anything from coding to marketing to a trade. Acquiring valuable skills makes you more employable or able to start a business, boosting your earning power.

Financial Literacy: Read personal finance books, take courses, or follow credible financial mentors. Understanding how money works (budgeting, taxes, basic economics, investing fundamentals) will pay dividends for the rest of your life.

Habits and Discipline: Cultivate good financial habits such as budgeting, saving a portion of your income, and avoiding impulsive spending. Building discipline early means you'll actually have money available to invest later.

Mindset and Health: Expand your mindset by surrounding yourself with positive influences and setting ambitious goals. Also, invest in your health because without physical and mental well-being, it's hard to sustain any wealth-building journey.

At this stage, your **time and energy** are the primary investments (with small amounts of money for courses or books as needed). The payoff is that you become a more capable earner and smarter investor.

Until you have something valuable to offer the world (skills, knowledge, labor), you can't expect meaningful financial returns. Level 1 creates the human capital that makes every later investment more effective.

Level 2: Invest in Your Own Business or Hustle

Once you've invested in yourself, the next step is to invest in something you **control**, i.e., your own enterprise or side hustle. This could mean starting a small business, or simply reinvesting in your current job or freelance gig to boost your income. By **Level 2**, you are essentially using money to directly create more money under your own direction. There's a great advantage here: you can often achieve returns in your own business far greater than in passive investments, and you gain firsthand experience in how capital can multiply when managed well.

For example, suppose you run a small online store, you might reinvest profits into **inventory** (allowing you to sell more) or **marketing** (bringing in new customers).

If you're a content creator, you could invest in a better camera or editing software to improve quality and grow your audience.

If you're a mechanic, buying more advanced tools or equipment could let you handle bigger jobs faster. All these are investments aimed at increasing your revenue. This stage is like your personal lab for learning to make money grow, you get to see directly how an extra $1,000 put into the right area can turn into $2,000, $5,000, etc., through increased sales or efficiency.

Here's a truth to remember: **If you can't multiply $1,000 in your own hands, why expect someone else to do it for you?** Investing in your own hustle tests and teaches your ability to generate returns. It's often said that entrepreneurs and self-employed individuals have high odds of building wealth. Indeed, statistics show self-employed people represent more than 20% of workers but account for two-thirds of millionaires.

The Millionaire Next Door study found that many millionaires got rich by owning businesses or being their own boss, not by salaries alone. Even if you don't want to start a company, treat your career or side gig with an entrepreneurial mindset: **reinvest in yourself and your work**. The lessons and returns from Level 2 will form the confidence and capital to tackle more outside investments later.

Level 3: Invest in Other People's Businesses

Now that you've built yourself up and learned to grow money in a venture you control, you're ready to invest in things you **don't control, namely**, other people's businesses. This is the level most folks mean by "investing": putting your money into stocks, funds, or perhaps local businesses, with the aim of earning returns as those enterprises prosper.

- **The Stock Market (start simple):** The stock market lets you buy a piece of large companies and benefit from their growth. For beginners, a smart approach is to **start with index funds** rather than picking individual stocks. An index fund is essentially a basket of many top companies bundled together. For example, an S&P 500 index fund gives you tiny ownership of 500 leading companies in one purchase. Why index funds? They offer built-in diversification across many companies, charge low fees, and have a long track record of solid performance. In fact, broad index funds often beat most actively managed mutual funds over the long run. By simply tracking the market, an index fund spares you from trying to guess "winning" stocks. Data shows that around 65% of professional fund managers underperform the market over 20-year spans, with virtually no category of active funds reliably beating indexes beyond 15 years. Index investing is also easy to manage (you don't need to constantly trade or research every company) and very cost-effective (many index funds charge near-zero annual fees). As a result, index funds have exploded in popularity. By the end of 2023, the total assets in U.S. passive index funds actually surpassed those in active funds for the first time. If you're new to stocks, consider making a simple index fund (or a few) the core of your portfolio. You'll get exposure to the growth of hundreds of businesses, essentially saying: "I believe the economy as a whole will grow over time, and I want my money to ride that wave." And historically, that's been a good bet because the U.S. market's 10% annual return means long-term stock investors have significantly grown their wealth and beat inflation.

- **Small Business and Local Ventures:** Beyond public stocks, you might find opportunities to invest in **private businesses**. It could be your friend's startup, a family member's expanding restaurant, or a local real estate development. These can offer much higher returns than the stock market, but they come with substantially higher risk and less liquidity (your money might be locked up, and the chance of failure is greater).

For instance, I've personally seen small venture investments that paid monthly returns of 10% or more an astonishing yield but those were speculative deals and I only committed what I could afford to lose, while making sure to **diversify** into different ventures.

The key here is diversification: don't put all your money in one business or one friend's idea. Spread your risk. Perhaps allocate a modest portion of your portfolio to these high-risk, high reward plays if you come across promising opportunities, but keep the bulk of your investments in more proven, liquid assets (like diversified stocks or bonds).

If you invest in a small business, do your homework: Understand the business model, the market, and the terms of your investment (ownership share, profit share, etc.). And only invest money you could mentally handle losing, because not all small businesses succeed. When they do succeed, however, you not only earn an excellent return, but you also get the satisfaction of helping grow someone's dream.

Level 3 is exciting, because now your money can start earning money in the background without your daily effort. Remember, though, that you're handing over control to others (corporate CEOs, fund managers, or business partners). That's why we built Levels 1 and 2

First, you have the knowledge and financial stability to navigate the market wisely.

By investing in a mix of other people's businesses (with an emphasis on diversified, high-quality assets), you set the stage for solid growth. Just always keep in mind the classic advice: **"Don't put all your eggs in one basket."**

A well-diversified portfolio across many companies and asset types will, on average, yield higher long-term returns with lower risk of any one failure derailing you. Spread your bets intelligently and let time and compound interest do their magic.

Level 4: Invest in People

This is one of the most powerful and frequently underestimated forms of investment. **Level 4 is about investing in relationships and teams**. No one truly achieves great wealth alone.

At some point, your success will be accelerated (or hindered) by the people around you: your mentors, peers, employees, partners, and community.

"You are the average of the five people you spend the most time with." This adage was coined by motivational speaker Jim Rohn.

Bottom line: If you aspire to be a millionaire, then **surround yourself with successful, driven people, ideally those who are where you want to be.** Their habits, knowledge, and networks will rub off on you.

If all your friends are financially irresponsible or have no ambition, guess what? It's going to be extremely hard for you to break out and build wealth. On the other hand, if you regularly interact with folks who are earning six-figure incomes, running businesses, or investing successfully, you'll learn from their experiences and elevate your own game.

In my own journey, I found that who I spent time with dramatically influenced my mindset. It's not about dumping old friends; it's about actively seeking out mentors and peers who

challenge you to grow. Networking isn't just career fluff; it's a real investment in your future success.

Companies with outstanding workplace culture ("100 Best Companies to Work For") dramatically outperform the broader market, achieving ~3175% stock returns over 27 years compared to ~907% for the overall Russell 1000 index (1998 2024). That's a 3.5× cumulative performance edge, underscoring how investing in people pays off financially. In other words, businesses that **treat their employees as if they are their greatest asset** tend to thrive and deliver superior returns to investors.

This isn't just correlation; there's a causal story: high-trust, inclusive, and development-focused work cultures drive lower turnover, higher innovation, and extra employee effort, which all boost the bottom line. Academic research reinforces this idea.

A 2024 analysis by RAND (Research and Development) economists found that companies making "high-quality, substantive investments" (higher wages, training, growth opportunities) in their frontline workers saw significantly higher stock performance. They concluded that if an investor held such employee-focused companies for 30 years, their returns could be roughly **double** what they'd get from less employee-friendly firms. The takeaway for us at an individual level: **Investing in people creates a virtuous cycle of wealth.**

So how can you apply Level 4? If you run a business or lead a team, invest in your people. Hire good people, pay them fairly, mentor them, and give them opportunities to grow. The more you lift up others, the more they will lift you. Your collective success will expand.

If you're not a business owner, you can still invest in the relationships around your financial life. Maybe it's partnering with someone who has skills you lack, or pooling resources with peers to achieve bigger goals (like real estate or a startup). It could even be as simple as sharing knowledge by forming an investment club or attending meetups with like-minded wealth builders. Also, **don't forget your family,** investing time in teaching your children or siblings about finance can multiply your family's generational wealth.

In business and in life, people truly are your greatest asset. The fastest way to become a billionaire, as the saying goes, is to **help one billion people** or more.

Level 4 reminds us that wealth is a team sport. By cultivating a strong network and supportive community, you dramatically accelerate your journey to financial freedom and amplify the scale of what you can achieve.

Level 5: Invest in Tools and Systems (Your Lifestyle)

By the time you've progressed through Levels 1 to 4, you've likely got multiple things going on: career, business, investments, and teams. Level 5 is about **optimizing for efficiency and scale**. In other words, invest in the tools, technology, and systems that will make your wealth-building machine run faster and smoother. Think of this as investing in your productive capacity and time. Every minute or dollar you save via a good system is a minute or dollar you can redeploy to grow or enjoy life.

One aspect is upgrading your tools to save time. This can be as straightforward as buying better hardware or software for your work. I'll give a personal example: I used to toil for hours on spreadsheets using a small laptop screen. It worked, but it was slow going. Eventually, I spent some money on two large monitors for my home office. The impact was instant; my productivity doubled overnight. I could see more data at once, multitask without switching windows, and experienced far less fatigue. It may sound trivial, but studies confirm this kind of boost.

Research by Microsoft found that moving from a single monitor to a dual-monitor setup can increase productivity by anywhere **from 9% up to 50%,** and other consultants reported an average 42% productivity gain for multi-screen users. That is huge!

Essentially, I was able to do two days of work in one, simply by using a better tool! In the same vein, when I finally invested in a good power drill for my home renovation side hustle, tasks that took an hour of sweat with a screwdriver were done in minutes. The lesson: do not skimp on tools that save you time and improve quality. Whether it's a faster laptop, better internet service, premium software, or hiring an assistant, these are not mere expenses; they are **investments in efficiency** that often pay for themselves quickly. Time is money, and any tool that gives you back time increases the rate at which you can earn and grow your money.

Another aspect of Level 5 is **automation and systems**. As you grow, look for ways to automate repetitive tasks and create processes that can scale. For example, if you have a business, you might invest in an e-commerce platform that handles orders and payments automatically, or in customer relationship management (CRM) software that streamlines marketing.

If managing your personal finances has become cumbersome, you could set up automated transfers to your investment accounts and use budgeting apps that track everything for you. Some people at this stage even invest in lifestyle upgrades that, while seeming like luxuries, actually buy back hours of their life. This might look like paying for a laundry or cleaning service so you can spend those hours on building their business or simply recharging (preventing burnout).

The underlying principle is **identify bottlenecks or drags on your time, and spend money to fix them.** It can feel strange to spend on “convenience” if you’re naturally frugal, but remember that your time has become very valuable. If you free up five hours a week by outsourcing a task, and you use that time to learn a new skill or manage your investments, the returns can far exceed the cost. At Level 5, you’re optimizing your lifestyle for wealth-building. Every system and tool in your life should be contributing to your goals or freeing you to focus on what truly matters (whether that’s further wealth or time with loved ones).

By investing in tools and systems, you effectively create a **money-making machine that can run more and more on its own.** This enables you to handle more wealth without a proportional increase in stress or workload. It’s how investors and entrepreneurs magnify their impact.

Imagine trying to oversee a portfolio of 10 rental properties without any property management software or help it would be chaos. But with proper systems, that same portfolio can be managed within a few hours a month. Thus, Level 5 completes the wealth journey: you’ve gone from improving yourself, to your business, to external investments, to networks, and finally to optimizing everything so that your money works at the highest possible rate while your involvement per dollar earned decreases.

Why Investing Matters

You might be thinking, “All these levels and strategies… is investing really worth all this effort?” The answer is a resounding **yes**, for several important reasons:

Building Capital Faster: Investing is the engine that can turn modest savings into serious wealth over time. If you simply save money under a mattress or in a basic bank account, it will not grow. Investing is what multiplies your money.

An example? $10,000 invested in a broad stock index 30 years ago would be worth well over $150,000 today (assuming ~10% annual returns), whereas $10,000 sitting in cash would still be $10,000 actually, much less in buying power due to inflation. In one inspiring real-world story, a U.S. president (long before he was president) invested just $2,000 in the stock market over 100 years ago; today, thanks to a century of compounding, that stake has grown to over $150 million. **That** is the astounding potential of long-term investing. It takes you from the linear path of trading hours for dollars and puts you on the exponential curve of wealth growth.

Beating Inflation: Inflation is the gradual increase in prices (and decrease in money's purchasing power) that happens in the economy. Even "low" inflation, say 3% per year, will erode the value of money significantly over decades (at 3%, **prices double every ~24 years**, meaning your dollar buys half as much in 24 years as it does today). If you don't invest, inflation is like a slow leak draining away your wealth. Investing allows you to **outpace inflation** by earning returns higher than the inflation rate. Historically, assets like stocks, real estate, and even bonds (in normal times) provide returns above inflation, so your money grows in real terms. In short, you need to invest just to stay ahead of the rising cost of living and maintain the value of your hard-earned money.

Creating Passive Income (Cash Flow): The right investments can generate income **for you even when you're not actively working**.

For instance, stocks pay dividends, bonds pay interest, and rental properties pay you rent, this is cash flow that can supplement or eventually replace your salary.

A steady $500 per month from investments might cover your utilities; $3,000 per month might cover your rent or allow you to go part-time at work. Investing is the cornerstone of the Financial Independence, Retire Early (FIRE) movement, where people accumulate enough assets to live off the investment income and quit traditional work decades early.

Whether or not FIRE is your goal, having investment income gives you **freedom and flexibility**. It's money coming in 24/7, even while you sleep or travel. Ultimately, enough passive income can fund your lifestyle entirely, which is the definition of financial freedom.

Retiring (or Reaching Goals) Early: Building on the above, investing is what makes early retirement or big life goals achievable in a timely manner. If you hope to retire comfortably, you simply won't get there by stashing a bit of cash in a checking account each month; you must get growth on those savings.

Thanks to the power of compounding, **the earlier and more consistently you invest, the sooner you can reach major financial milestones** like buying a home, paying for your kids' college, or retiring.

For example, if you invest $500 a month, earning ~8% annually starting at age 25, by age 55, you could have around $750,000. Delay starting until 35, and you'd have only about $300,000 by 55, which is a huge difference. Investing literally buys you time in terms of life choices. It can enable you to retire at 55 instead of 65, or to take a sabbatical or change careers without financial worry. It's the ticket to options in life.

Leaving a Legacy: Finally, investing is how you create generational wealth or support causes you care about. By growing an estate over your lifetime, you can set up your family for a better future by perhaps funding your children's down payments on homes, or creating an inheritance that gives your grandchildren a head start. Beyond family, your investments could fund charitable endowments, scholarships, or any legacy you envision. One famous example: Benjamin Franklin (Not an investor in stocks, but a savvy money manager of his era) left about £1,000 in a trust in the 1790s to grow for 200 years; through compound interest, it turned into millions, which then funded public projects in Boston and Philadelphia.

When you invest, your money outlives you. It continues to work and has an impact even when you're gone. That's a powerful reason to take it seriously.

In summary, **investing matters because it is the bridge between working for money and having money work for you.** It's the only realistic way to achieve substantial wealth on an average income, and the sooner you begin, the more of an ally time becomes. By steadily investing and moving through the "five levels," you will accumulate capital, shield yourself from inflation, generate income streams, and gain the freedom to design your life.

One of the most motivating tales I know is the incredible effect of long-term compounding. As mentioned, a modest $2,000 investment made over a century ago grew into over $150 million today. That kind of growth seems almost magical, but it's just math and patience the magic of compound interest. Albert Einstein called compound interest the "8th wonder of the world" for good reason. Whether or not that specific story inspires you, I hope the framework and principles we've discussed do.

Final Thoughts: Investing isn't just stock picks or real estate deals; it's a holistic strategy and structure for wealth-building. If you follow the Five Levels of Investment through each stage of your life, you will position yourself to grow faster, avoid major setbacks, and build real, lasting wealth.

Start by investing in yourself (build your earning ability and knowledge). Then invest in your own ventures (prove to yourself you can grow money). Branch out to invest in the wider markets and others' businesses (letting your money ride the broader economy). Invest in people and relationships (multiplying your opportunities and impact). Finally, invest in tools and systems (to optimize and scale your efforts).

This is how you build wealth one level at a time, one brick at a time.

By being intentional and progressive, you transform investing from a gamble into a reliable wealth engine.

The levels also serve as a check and balance: whenever you feel uncertain, you can always "return" to a prior level. Feeling like your stock picks are shaky? Go back to Level 1 and 2, invest in learning more or boosting your income so you have more capital to invest.

Each level reinforces the others. In the end, a strong you, combined with smart investments and great people around, supported by efficient systems, is an unbeatable combination. That's the life-changing realization I had on my journey, and I hope it serves you well, too.

Here's to having not just money that works, but **a life that works for you** with money as a powerful tool, not a limitation. Happy investing, and enjoy watching your money start working for you!

CHAPTER SIX: CREDIT

When I first arrived in the United States, the concept of **credit** was completely foreign to me. I had no understanding of how to build or maintain good credit. In the United States of America's financial system, however, credit plays a central role in nearly every major financial decision: from renting an apartment to buying a car or house.

As a new immigrant with no credit history, I soon learned I was essentially invisible to lenders. This chapter chronicles my journey from having no credit and later bad credit to rebuilding a solid credit score, and the hard lessons learned along the way.

I am sharing this with you to help you avoid some of the very hard-won and humbling mistakes I made so you can avoid them, and the adversity that ignorance and impulsive credit- impacting actions can create in your life.

Take heed and build your credit the right way!

My First Steps into the Credit World

Eager to establish myself financially, I opened my first U.S. bank account at a small regional bank (Independent Bank). Confidently, I asked them for a credit card. To my surprise, they refused. I was over 21 and a college graduate, so I believed I should be eligible. What I didn't realize is that without any credit history, banks see you as a high-risk or unknown borrower.

As a newcomer with no credit record, I didn't yet have a score to prove my creditworthiness. In the U.S., having no credit is not the same as having bad credit, but it does pose challenges until you start building a credit history.

A friend suggested I try a **credit union** instead, since they are often more flexible with new borrowers. Following that advice, I joined a credit union, and they approved me for a **secured credit card**. A secured card required me to deposit $500 of my own money. In exchange, they gave me a credit card with a $500 limit. (In general, secured credit cards require an upfront security deposit, often between $200 to $2,000, which typically becomes your credit line.)

The credit union officer explained that if I used the card responsibly for one year, making every payment on time, they would then release my $500 collateral and convert it to a regular unsecured credit card. Some credit unions even **upgrade secured cards to unsecured after 12 months** of on-time payments, and that's exactly what happened in my case.

After a year of never missing a payment, the credit union returned my deposit and increased my credit limit to $1,000 on an unsecured card.

So now I finally have a credit card, but I still don't really understand how to manage it wisely. I had achieved the goal of getting credit, yet I was about to learn the painful lesson that **having credit available is not the same as using it correctly.**

Mistakes, Debt, and Harsh Lessons

After graduating and during a period of job-hunting, my financial discipline was nearly zero. I had no budget and little understanding of debt. Inevitably, I **maxed out** that $1,000 credit card very quickly.

With no steady income yet, I used the card for day-to-day living expenses until it hit the limit. Each month, I sent in at least the minimum payment due, thinking that meant I was being responsible and keeping the account in good standing. Unfortunately, I didn't realize that paying only the minimum is a **debt trap**. Minimum payments are usually set very low, often around 2% of the balance, which means the payment barely covers the interest on the debt.

In fact, credit card issuers design minimum payments so that you pay just a little more than that month's interest, resulting in the principal balance shrinking by only a few dollars. I was ignorant of this. I'd see my payment posted and assume I was handling the card correctly, while in reality, 90% of my minimum payments were going straight to interest charges and hardly denting the balance.

Compounding this, the **interest rate** on the card was extremely high, somewhere between 20% and 27% annual percentage rate (APR). Many credit cards carry interest rates in the 20%+ range, especially for those with limited or poor credit.

Carrying a balance at such a high interest means that the debt grows rapidly. I was essentially treading water or even sinking deeper in debt each month, even though I was making payments. This was a harsh lesson: just paying the minimum on a maxed-out card with a 25% APR is a recipe for perpetual debt.

I learned that if you only pay the minimum on a high-interest card, **it could take years, even decades, to pay off** the balance (if ever) because interest keeps accumulating. Take my lesson as your warning on this one!

Driving Deeper into Debt

Eventually, I did land my first full-time job. By then, I was married and we had a young daughter. Living in an area with limited public transportation, owning reliable vehicles was practically a necessity for us. My old car was on its last legs, constantly breaking down. With my new employment income, I decided to take out a car loan of $20,000 to purchase a better car. In hindsight, this decision was well-intentioned but flawed: instead of buying one reliable car with the loan, I thought it would be smart to get two used cars (one for myself and one for my wife,) each under $10,000. My reasoning was that we'd both have transportation for the price of one new car.

What I didn't fully grasp was that I was **doubling our financial risk**. Now we had two cars to maintain, two cars depreciating, and a $20k debt to service on a limited income.

Not long after this decision was made, life threw us a curveball. About a year into my job, the grant funding for my position ran out, and I was laid off. Overnight, our household went from two incomes (my job and my wife's part-time work) down to no income, since my wife had to leave work around the same time due to pregnancy complications with our second child.

With no money coming into the household, I inevitably fell behind on the car loan payments. I missed three months of payments in a row while we were scrambling to stay afloat. It wasn't long before I realized that my ability to keep swimming against the current of poor credit decisions would soon bring our family to the brink of bankruptcy.

A Turning Point: Repossession and Rock Bottom

One chilly December morning in 2013, I walked outside planning to leave for a side gig I was trying (selling insurance on commission) And both of our cars were gone from the driveway. My heart dropped I thought they had been stolen. After a frantic moment, I called the bank through which they were financed. They confirmed the grim truth: both vehicles had been repossessed in the early hours of the morning due to the missed payments.

In the United States, when you default on a car loan, the lender has the right to take back the vehicle, often without warning, once you are sufficiently delinquent (Sometimes even one missed payment can trigger a repossession, though lenders might wait 60-90 days). We had missed three, so the hammer came down hard.

It's hard to express in words how truly devastating this was. We suddenly had no transportation, which was not only a personal blow but it also meant I instantly lost my job opportunity as an insurance agent that job absolutely required a car to visit clients. The timing couldn't have been worse: my wife was pregnant with our second child, our first was a toddler, and now we were stranded.

Emotions in our household were at a breaking point; our marriage was under immense strain as we faced this crisis. On top of the immediate practical nightmare, our credit scores were in freefall.

A repossession is a major derogatory mark on your credit report, it stays on the report for up to seven years and can easily shave 100 points or more off your score. Ours plummeted into the low 400s, which is an extremely poor credit range (to give context, anything under 580 is considered "poor" credit). I wouldn't be surprised if our scores had dropped below 400 at the worst point. We had truly hit **rock bottom** financially: no cars, no job, growing debt, a new baby on the way, and a credit score in the gutter.

In that dark period, I felt like I had failed my family. It seemed almost impossible to climb out. But sometimes rock bottom becomes the solid foundation on which to rebuild. Out of desperation and with nowhere to go but up, I reached out to my pastor for guidance and support. That conversation turned out to be a turning point both in my finances and my faith.

Finding Light: My Financial Education

My pastor introduced me to something called Dave Ramsey's Financial Peace University (FPU). The church had just acquired the FPU program materials, and he suggested that I participate. In fact, he asked if I would be willing to volunteer as the class facilitator since I was so eager to turn my finances around.

Despite my own financial turmoil (or rather because of it), I agreed to facilitate the weekly FPU classes at the church. This meant I had to learn the material in order to guide discussions. Week by week, lesson by lesson, I absorbed the basics of budgeting, saving, getting out of debt, and understanding credit.

Financial Peace University is a nine-lesson personal finance course that teaches participants how to save for emergencies, budget effectively, pay off debt quickly, spend wisely, and invest for the future.

It's a faith-based, common-sense program that emphasizes living on a budget, cutting up credit cards, and using cash. Dave Ramsey is famously anti-credit-card, advocating that people avoid debt altogether.

While I didn't follow all of the Ramsey philosophies to the letter (more on that later), the program was a lifeline for instilling financial discipline. Facilitating the class forced me to confront my own bad habits.

I started making a budget for the first time. My wife and I began having honest conversations about money, planning out each dollar (the Ramsey approach uses the **"zero-based budget,"** meaning you give every dollar a job each month).

We built a small emergency fund as the class instructed for "Baby Step 1," and we systematically worked on the "debt snowball" to tackle smaller debts first.

One of the most eye-opening exercises was pulling my credit reports to see exactly what shape things were in. Through FPU, I learned about the official site AnnualCreditReport.com, where you can get your credit reports for free.

Under U.S. law, each person can get one free report per year from each of the three bureaus. I went to that site and requested my full credit report from all three major credit bureaus (Experian, Equifax, and TransUnion). Seeing that report in black and white was humbling. It listed the credit card I had maxed out (showing very high utilization and a history of only minimum payments), several accounts in **collections** (small medical bills and an old utility bill forgotten about), and, of course, the big **auto loan**, which was now showing as a **charge-off** after the repossession.

A charge-off means the lender has given up on collecting the full amount and written it off as a loss. It's about as bad as a delinquency can get on a report, aside from bankruptcy or foreclosure. No wonder my credit score was 460.

The good news was that by educating myself, I at least had a plan. The hopelessness started to fade as I replaced it with concrete steps for rebuilding credit and financial stability. If you see yourself in this story, I encourage you to keep reading on to start putting your own action plan in place.

The Rebuilding Process

The road to restoring my credit was long (several years) and required both financial discipline and some strategic maneuvers to address the negative items on my credit report. I essentially had to rebuild my credit score and my financial stability from scratch, cleaning up the past mistakes while slowly adding positive information to outweigh the bad. Here is exactly how I approached it:

1. Cleaning up **smaller derogatory items:** I had a few minor collections on my report (for example, a utility bill under $200 that went to collections when I moved, and a small medical co-pay). My first step was to **pay off or settle any collections under $200.** This was advice I picked up from online research and forums: small collections ("nuisance" accounts) are sometimes ignored by newer scoring models, but I didn't want any past-due accounts at all if I could help it. I either paid these in full or negotiated a settlement and, in some cases, requested a "pay for delete" (where the collector agrees to remove the item from your credit report if you pay it. Not all will do this, but it doesn't hurt to ask. Getting rid of these small collections removed some of the easiest "black marks" on my report.

2. Disputing **errors and outdated information:** Next, I **wrote letters to the credit bureaus** to remove old inquiries and any errors I spotted. Credit inquiries (from when you apply for credit) only impact your score for about a year and fall off your report after two years, but I had a lot of hard inquiries from those desperate times of applying for loans and cards.

I used template letters I found online. There are many examples of free "credit inquiry removal letters," or you can use AI to write your own. I used these letters to dispute any outdated negative items that, by law, should have been removed. Most negative marks can stay on your record for seven years. Over the course of a couple of months, I mailed out over 50 letters to creditors, collection agencies, and the credit bureaus, essentially pleading my case or requesting verification of debts. Looking back, this was a shotgun approach to credit repair, but it did pay off. Many inquiries were removed as a result (some creditors didn't bother to verify them when challenged), and a couple of small collection accounts that I had paid got updated or deleted. My credit score moved from the miserable 460 range up to around the 530s in a matter of months. Still bad, but it signaled progress.

3. Tackling the **big default (the car loan charge-off):** The elephant in the room on my credit report was the ~$20,000 auto loan charge-off from the repossession. I knew this major derogatory item would weigh down my score until it was resolved or aged off.

At this time, I simply **could not afford** to pay it off or settle it, as I was barely scraping by and focusing on keeping current on new obligations. After some soul-searching, I made the hard decision to **let that charge-off sit unpaid.**

I basically ignored the collection calls on it and decided to focus on rebuilding positive credit instead of throwing money (which I didn't have) at a massive debt that was already charged off. My rationale was that negative items hurt less as they age, and after 7 years, they fall off the report entirely. In my case, I got a bit lucky; after about 5 years, I was able to **petition the credit bureaus to remove the repossession.**

I wrote dispute letters arguing that the account was too old or that the information was inaccurate in some way (I don't exactly recall the argument I used. Perhaps I claimed the account age was past the statute of limitations). Whether by policy or simply by the creditor not verifying it when the dispute was filed, the repossession record was removed around the 5-year mark.

When that huge black mark finally dropped off, my credit score **jumped into the mid-600s** (around 650). That was an enormous relief and a turning point; I had gone from the 400s to the 600s, leaving the “very poor” credit tier and entering the “fair/good” range.

Throughout this rebuilding phase, I **lived on a cash budget** as much as possible (Thanks to the habits learned from Financial Peace University). We used the envelope system for groceries, gas, etc., to avoid incurring new debt. I did keep one credit card open (That same credit union card, now unsecured with a $1k limit) to have some active credit history, but I was extremely careful with it. I was using it for a small purchase and paying it off in full occasionally, just to show activity.

By 2015, two years after the repossession, my credit was stabilized in the mid-600s. I was employed steadily as an auditor. It was a stable, salaried job, and with the negative items aging, I could finally start playing offense with a strategic credit-building plan, rather than just defense.

Strategic Credit Building Begins

Once my wife and I had righted the ship financially both of us working steady jobs and living within our means we moved into the next phase: **building good credit strategically.** We didn’t want to just escape “bad credit”; we wanted to proactively earn great credit scores for the future.

This part of the journey took several more years (credit improvement is usually a marathon, not a sprint), but by employing smart strategies consistently, we saw dramatic improvements. Here are the key strategies we used:

1) **Maintaining low credit utilization on two credit cards:** We decided to keep **only two primary credit card accounts** open (One in my name and one in my wife's name), rather than opening a bunch of new credit lines. The logic was to focus on a couple of cards and manage them well. On each card, we maintained the balance at **under 30% of the credit limit** at all times. For example, if a card had a $1000 limit, we'd never carry more than about $300 as a balance on it. Keeping your **credit utilization ratio** (balance-to-limit percentage) below about 30% is a commonly recommended practice because utilization above 30% can start to drag down your score. In fact, people with excellent credit often use less than 10% of their available credit, but staying under 30% is a widely cited guideline. The Consumer Financial Protection Bureau (CFPB), a government agency, also suggests keeping utilization low to help improve your credit score. By limiting our spending on each card, or paying mid-cycle if we had to, we made sure high utilization would never be an issue on our reports.

2) **Requesting credit limit increases instead of new credit:** Rather than applying for new credit cards (which would ding our credit with hard inquiries and reset the "average age" of accounts, we periodically requested credit line increases on our existing cards. The idea was to gradually increase our available credit on the cards we already had, which further lowers the utilization percentage without the downside of new accounts. For instance, after some months of on-time payments, I called the credit union and asked if they could raise my credit limit from $1,000 to $2,000.

They did so with only a soft pull inquiry (Some issuers might do a hard pull, meaning that they do an inquiry as if you are getting a new credit card, but mine did not). The impact it had on my utilization rate was immediate: a $300 balance is 30% of $1,000, but only 15% of $2,000. As Capital One notes, a higher credit limit can help your credit score as long as you don't increase your spending, because it improves your utilization ratio. We followed this principle carefully.

3) **Reporting our rent payments.** One creative tool we used was a rent-reporting service. We were renters at the time, and normally, rent payments do not show up on credit reports (credit bureaus usually only track debt payments like loans, credit cards, etc.). However, there are third-party services that will report your on-time rent payments to the major credit bureaus, effectively turning your rent history into a tradeline on your credit report. We signed up for a service (for a small fee) that verified our rent payments each month and sent that data to Experian and TransUnion. This added a positive payment history to our credit files for something we were doing anyway paying rent. Reporting rent doesn't impact your score as heavily as a loan or card might, but it can help build a thicker credit file for someone with limited accounts. Since we had years of perfect rent payments, it was a bonus to get credit for it (pun intended).

4) **Never missing a payment (the 100% on-time streak):** By this point, we were extremely strict about paying every single bill on time, every time. Payment history is the number one factor in credit scores (worth about 35% of your FICO score), and any late payment can hurt you, so we set up automatic payments and reminders to ensure we

didn't slip up. Even a single 30-day late payment can knock dozens of points off your score, so we treated due dates as sacred. This consistent positive payment history began to populate our credit reports and outweighed the old negatives as they aged off.

5) **Credit repair help for my wife:** We also invested in a credit expert service to assist with cleaning up my wife's credit report. She had some lingering issues from years past, including some late student loan payments and an old collection. We paid a credit repair company for a few months to send dispute letters on her behalf and coach us on steps to raise her score. I was skeptical, but to their credit (again, pun intended), they did help her remove a couple of negative items. I'd caution others: you can often do whatever a credit repair agency does by yourself, but in our case, we were busy, and I was focusing on mine while the service helped with hers.

Over the next few years of practicing these habits, our credit scores steadily rose. I watched my own FICO score go from the 600s to the upper 700s. Eventually, I peeked around a 750+ score, which is considered very good credit (generally 740 and above is "very good," and 800+ is "excellent").

My wife's score also climbed into the 700s after her report was cleaned up and she maintained perfect payments. I never did hit the 800 club, but that was okay, because we had reached our goal of restoring our creditworthiness.

We were able to progress from not being able to qualify for a basic credit card and having sub-500 credit scores to scores in the 700s, which opened the door to better interest rates and bigger financial opportunities.

How long did this take? A total of about 7 years of patient work from the darkest point to the point where I felt our credit was strong again. However, the journey of restoring our credit taught us so much more than just how to raise a FICO number, as I will share with you next.

Lessons Learned and What Matters Most

Looking back, this credit journey was difficult but incredibly educational. The mistakes I made now serve as lessons that I share with others.

Here are the biggest takeaways and why they matter:

1.) **Good credit reduces the cost of debt.** One of the most powerful lessons is that having a good (or excellent) credit score will save you a lot of money over your lifetime. Lenders offer **much lower interest rates** and better terms to borrowers with strong credit. For example, someone with a 750 score might get a car loan at 4% interest, whereas someone with a 600 score could be charged 10% or more for the same loan. Over the years, that difference could mean paying thousands more in interest for the lower-score borrower. In mortgages, the difference is even more staggering: a lower credit score can literally cost tens of thousands of extra dollars in interest.

2.) **Higher credit scores = lower rates = big savings**. It's essentially a reward for managing credit well: you become less costly to lend to. I experienced both sides of this. When my score was in the 400s, I couldn't get approved for anything, and if I did, it was a predatory 29% interest type of situation. Now with scores in the 700s, I get 0% financing offers in the mail and low-rate pre-approvals. The financial peace of mind (and money saved) from good credit is very real.

3.) **Strong income supports strong credit.** Credit-building isn't just about the credit accounts; it's also heavily dependent on your overall financial stability. One hard truth we learned is that you need consistent cash flow to pay down debts, make on-time payments, and avoid relying on credit for emergencies. In my case, things started improving once I had a steady job and we were living on a budget. A budget only works if there's income to budget with! When I was unemployed or underemployed, even with the best intentions, I couldn't pay bills on time, which wrecked my credit. While income doesn't directly show up on a credit report, it indirectly underpins everything.

4.) **Living within our means** (a.k.a. spending less than you earn.) Adopting this discipline allowed us to slowly but surely improve our credit profile. If you're trying to rebuild credit, also work on improving your income if possible whether through a better job, side hustle, or cutting expenses to free up cash. It makes all the difference, because money problems often lead to credit problems. Once we had decent salaries, we could attack our debts aggressively and never miss payments, which in turn boosted our scores.

5.) **Understand what drives your credit score.** Credit scores (like the FICO score) may seem mysterious, but they actually follow a known formula. Educating myself on the components of a credit score was a gamechanger. Here's a quick breakdown of FICO score factors:

Note: Key factors make up a FICO credit score. Payment history and amounts owed (utilization) carry the most weight.

Anatomy of a Credit Score

Payment History (35%): This is the biggest slice. It tracks whether you pay your bills on time. Late payments, defaults, collections, and bankruptcies devastate this category. Consistent on-time payments, even if just the minimum, help a lot. Our turnaround hinged on never being late again.

Amounts Owed / Credit Utilization (30%): This relates to how much debt you carry relative to your credit limits. High balances (especially if near your limits) hurt your score, while lower utilization helps. Try to keep utilization under 30% (even better, under 10% when possible). Paying down debt is one of the fastest ways to boost this part of your score.

Length of Credit History (15%): Creditors look at how long you've had credit accounts open. Older accounts (in good standing) are beneficial. This is why it can be smart to keep your oldest account open. In our case, my credit union card started in 2011, so by 2020, it gave me nearly nine years of history, which was a significant boost.

New Credit/Inquiries (10%): Opening several new accounts in a short time or having many hard inquiries can ding your score. We minimized new credit applications during rebuilding. Each time you apply for credit, your score might drop a few points temporarily.

We staggered any necessary inquiries and avoided the "apply for everything" panic that I did in my troubled times.

Credit Mix (10%): Having a mix of different types of credit (e.g., a credit card, an auto loan, maybe a mortgage or student loan) can help your score a little bit because it shows you can handle different kinds of debt. However, mix is a minor factor; you don't need to go out and get loans you don't need just for a diverse credit mix. We happened to eventually have an auto loan again and credit cards, which is a reasonable mix.

Knowing these factors guided our strategy: we focused heavily on payment history and utilization, since together they're two-thirds of the score. We were patient with the length of history, careful about new credit, and didn't worry too much about mix beyond ensuring we had at least one installment loan on record eventually.

Beyond the credit score itself - timing is everything!

Timing is indeed everything; build credit before you need it. Perhaps the most poignant lesson is that **credit takes time** to build, and if you wait until the moment you desperately need a good credit score, it's already too late.

Building credit is like planting a tree. The best time to do it was years ago; the second-best time is now. Don't wait until you're in a pinch to care about your credit score.

Many people (my past self-included) only start caring about their credit when they want to get a mortgage, car loan, or even rent an apartment, and then they discover their score is too low or nonexistent. By then, you can't magically fix it overnight. The key is to be proactive: start with small credit accounts, use them wisely, and build that positive history well *before* you plan to use credit for a major life event.

Even if you prefer to live debt-free (as I largely do now), it's wise to have a strong credit profile as a safety net and for life's necessities. I learned this the hard way.

I ignored credit as a young adult, only to find myself unable to get an apartment lease without a co-signer and paying high deposits for utilities because I had no credit. Later, when my credit was damaged, I got hit with outrageous interest rates.

Had I been more proactive in the beginning, I could have saved myself a lot of pain.

Finally, I learned that **credit is just one part of a bigger financial picture.** It intertwines with budgeting, saving, and planning. The journey from the 400s to the 700s took nearly seven years, but along the way, we developed habits that improved all aspects of our finances.

We now live on a budget, have an emergency fund to avoid future desperate credit use, and communicate about money openly. In a way, I'm grateful for the early hardships, because they forced me to gain financial wisdom I might have otherwise ignored. Today, my family's credit scores are healthy, our debt is under control (we avoid unnecessary debt entirely), and we have the knowledge to proactively keep our finances moving in a positive direction.

The climb out of the credit hole was steep and filled with setbacks, but reaching the summit seeing a 750 on my credit report and knowing we have financial options was incredibly rewarding. Good credit has given us the freedom to refinance our car at a low rate, qualify for a nice rental home (and soon a mortgage), and most importantly, never again be at the mercy of predatory lenders. The stress in our lives around money has been drastically reduced, while our quality of life has exponentially improved.

Make a commitment to healthy credit habits

In summary, credit can be a friend or foe. Treat it responsibly, and it will open doors and save you money; treat it recklessly and it can cost you dearly.

I've been on both sides of the credit coin, and I much prefer having good credit. The hard-earned peace of mind that comes with it, knowing we can handle an emergency or secure a loan if needed, is perhaps the greatest benefit of all. And that is something I will never take for granted again.

Sources: Good credit leads to lower borrowing costs; New immigrants often start with no credit history; Secured credit cards require a deposit and can convert to unsecured with on-time payments; Making only minimum payments means most of your money goes to interest; Average credit card APRs are very high (~20%+), making high balances costly; A car repossession stays on credit ~7 years and can drop your score by 100+ points; Financial Peace University teaches budgeting and debt payoff principles; Credit utilization should be kept under 30% (ideally under 10%); Rent-reporting services can help build credit history for renters; Credit score factors: 35% payment history, 30% amounts owed/utilization, 15% length, 10% new credit, 10% mix; Many people only realize the importance of credit when they need it for a loan or home proactive building is crucial.

CHAPTER SEVEN: TAXES

Optimizing Your Taxes to Optimize Personal Financial Planning

Taxes affect virtually every part of your financial life. In fact, taxes are often one of the largest expenses you will face over your lifetime, and without planning, they can rapidly erode your income, profits and accumulated wealth.

Every dollar paid in tax is a dollar no longer available to save or invest for your future goals. This is why tax considerations are essential in personal financial planning. By incorporating tax strategies into your plan, you ensure that more of your hard-earned money stays in your pocket, working for you rather than trading away your future financial stability to the IRS.

Importantly, tax planning isn't about evading taxes; it's about being efficient and proactive with the tax rules. The U.S. tax code provides many legal opportunities (deductions, credits, special accounts, etc.) that reward behaviors like saving for retirement, investing, owning a home, or starting a business. By taking advantage of these tax incentives and planning ahead, you can significantly boost your ability to build wealth over time.

As a tax preparation firm notes, advanced planning is necessary because without it, taxes can "rapidly erode profits and accumulated wealth." In short, understanding taxes and planning for them is a crucial part of any solid financial plan. It can mean the difference between just making money and actually keeping money to grow your wealth.

The Cumulative Power of Proper Tax Planning

One of the most compelling reasons to prioritize tax planning is the cumulative effect it has on your wealth. Year by year, smart tax moves may seem to yield modest savings a few hundred or a few thousand dollars here and there. But over decades, those savings can compound dramatically. Morningstar research illustrates this vividly: over a 40-year investment period, the drag of taxes on returns could cost a hypothetical investor almost $1 million in lost wealth.

In other words, two investors with identical portfolios could end up in very different places simply because one paid more taxes along the way than the other.

Smart tax planning recognizes that ***it's not just about what you make, it's about what you keep.***

By finding ways to defer or reduce taxes, you keep more money invested and working for you, which leads to greater growth over time. Even small adjustments can yield big results.

By making a few tax-savvy moves now, you could keep thousands more dollars of your income each year money that can be redirected into investments or savings. Each year's tax savings can be invested to generate investment returns, creating a snowball effect that accelerates your wealth-building.

To see the power of compounding in action, consider a simple scenario: if you invest a $6,500 tax refund or tax savings today and earn a 7% annual return, in 25 years that single sum could grow to around $35,000. Remember all we covered in our chapter on investments? Taking your tax savings to leverage into truly can pay dividends with added investment returns

Imagine doing this every year the long-term payoff is enormous. Similarly, using tax-advantaged accounts can turn small contributions into big nest eggs. For instance, contributing the maximum to a Health Savings Account just once (around $3,850 for a single person) at age 30 could grow into over $40,000 by age 65 (assuming a 7% return), all of it potentially tax-free for medical use.

These examples show how proper tax planning, when applied consistently, leads to significantly greater wealth over the long run. The bottom line: tax planning multiplies the impact of your other financial efforts: it boosts the net returns on your investments and the net income you get to keep from your work.

Key Tax Strategies to Build Wealth

Tax planning might sound technical, but it really boils down to common-sense strategies that anyone can use. Here are some of the most impactful tax strategies to help build wealth, especially for individuals and families in the $50,000 to $300,000 income range:

1.) Maximize Tax-Advantaged Retirement Plans

One of the simplest and most effective strategies is to contribute as much as you can to tax-advantaged retirement accounts like 401(k)s, 403(b)s, Traditional IRAs, and Roth IRAs. Contributions to traditional 401(k) or IRA accounts are tax-deferred, meaning they reduce your taxable income today (giving you an immediate tax break) and grow tax-deferred until retirement.

For example, if you're in the 22% federal tax bracket, contributing $5,000 to a traditional 401(k) saves you roughly $1,100 in federal taxes for the year. That's $1,100 more kept in your pocket (or rather, in your retirement account) instead of being paid in taxes.

Higher income earners get an even bigger absolute benefit. As one financial commentator quipped, there are few high earners who wouldn't benefit from deferring the maximum $22,500 (2024 limit) in a 401(k), because the upfront tax savings are so substantial.

Don't forget that many employers offer 401(k) matching contributions, which is something you should definitely take advantage of because it is essentially free money toward your retirement.

For those not covered by an employer plan or who want to save more, Traditional IRAs (if you fall under income limits for deductibility) provide similar tax-deferred growth. Even if you can't deduct an IRA contribution due to income, you may be able to do a Backdoor Roth IRA (contribute after-tax and then convert to Roth), which lets high earners put money into a Roth IRA indirectly.

Roth accounts (like a Roth IRA or Roth 401k) won't give a tax break today, but they grow completely tax-free, and qualified withdrawals in retirement are tax-free. With a Roth, you essentially pay taxes now so you can enjoy tax-free income later, which can be very powerful if you expect to be in a higher tax bracket down the road or want to avoid taxes on investment growth.

The key is to use these retirement vehicles fully: they either save taxes now or later, plus they shelter your investments from annual taxes, allowing more rapid compounding of interest on your money. Over decades, maximizing retirement contributions can be a cornerstone of both lowering lifetime taxes and accumulating wealth.

2.) Use Health Savings Accounts (the "Triple Tax" Benefit).

If you have access to a Health Savings Account (HSA) through a high-deductible health insurance plan, it can be another fantastic tax-advantaged tool for building wealth.

HSAs are often called the "triple tax benefit" account. Here's why:

a. contributions to an HSA are tax-deductible (or pre-tax), which lowers your taxable income.
b. the money in the HSA grows tax-free (any interest, dividends, or investment gains are not taxed); and
c. Withdrawals are tax-free as long as they are used for qualified medical expenses.

In other words, an HSA is the only investment account that is tax-free going in, growing, and coming out (for qualified medical needs).

Bonus: If you contribute via payroll deduction, HSA contributions also escape FICA payroll taxes, saving an additional 7.65% in Social Security/ Medicare tax.*Using an HSA for long-term wealth- building might sound odd since it's for healthcare expenses, but consider this strategy: contribute to your HSA each year (up to the annual limit), invest those funds for growth, and pay current medical costs out-of-pocket from your cash flow if you can. There's no "use it or lose it" rule; unlike FSAs, your Over time, you build a sizable medical nest egg that can cover healthcare in retirement (tax-free). And after age 65, you can withdraw HSA funds for any purpose (not just medical).

Those withdrawals will just be taxed like a Traditional IRA withdrawal (essentially turning into an extra retirement account if needed). The HSA's triple-tax advantage means it beats even a 401k or IRA in tax efficiency.

As a simple illustration, a one-time HSA contribution of about $3,800 at age 30 could grow to over $40,000 by age 65 (assuming a 7% return) and that entire amount could be spent on medical needs tax-free. In short, if you have an HSA option, take advantage of it. It's both a tax reduction and wealth-building

3.) Invest Tax-Efficiently (Capital Gains and Tax)

How you invest can have big tax implications, which in turn affect your net investment returns. Tax-efficient investing means structuring your investments to minimize taxes and the drag they cause on growth. Here are a few tips:

a.) Choose long-term over short-term gains: If you hold investments like stocks or mutual funds for over a year before selling, you qualify for long-term capital gains tax rates, which are much lower than ordinary income tax rates. Most people pay a 15% federal tax on long-term gains (20% if you're high income), versus potentially 22%, 24%, or 32%-plus if that same profit was taxed as short-term gain or regular income. In fact, lower-income investors may pay 0% tax on long-term capital gains up to certain income limits. By contrast, frequent trading that realizes short-term gains (or high-turnover funds that distribute taxable gains annually) can lead to unnecessary tax bills each year.

b.) Whenever possible, hold investments for the long term to get the tax break and keep more of your gains compounding.

c.) Use tax-efficient investment vehicles: If you have money in taxable brokerage accounts, consider using index funds or ETFs, which tend to be more tax-efficient than actively managed funds (they distribute fewer taxable gains).

d.) Also, municipal bonds pay interest that is tax-free federally (and state-tax-free if from your home state), which can benefit those in higher tax brackets.

e.) If you have stock investments with large gains, strategies like tax-loss harvesting (selling some investments at a loss to offset gains) can reduce capital gains tax exposure. Always be mindful of the tax consequences of rebalancing or selling investments. Sometimes, making a change can wait until an asset qualifies for long-term gain treatment, or it can be done in a tax-deferred account to avoid current tax.

f.) Avoid tax drag on investments: Over a lifetime, repeatedly paying even 15% or 20% tax on gains can significantly slow down the growth of your portfolio. As noted earlier, taxes create a drag that can cost hundreds of thousands over decades. To minimize this drag, keep high-tax investments in tax-sheltered accounts when possible. For example, interest from taxable bonds is best in an IRA/401 (k) (where it won't be taxed yearly), whereas stock index funds can be very tax-efficient in a taxable account.

The goal is to allocate assets optimally so that you aren't paying more tax than necessary while you grow your wealth. Every dollar not lost to tax is a dollar still compounding for you. As one advisory firm succinctly put it: "Every investment move should be evaluated for tax risk… A lifetime of investment decisions and their tax implications can have a powerful cumulative effect on your returns."

Leverage Tax Credits and Deductions

Tax credits and deductions are powerful tools to cut your tax bill and free up more money to invest or save. Tax deductions reduce your taxable income, which in turn reduces taxes owed (the value of a deduction depends on your tax bracket).

Tax credits, on the other hand, directly reduce your tax dollar-for-dollar (a $1,000 credit cuts your taxes by $1,000, regardless of your bracket).

It's important, especially for middle-income earners, to claim every tax break you're entitled to you might be surprised how much they can add up. As one publication notes, recent updates to tax laws expanded many breaks for middle-class taxpayers, so it's "vital for everyone… to claim all the tax breaks legally available to them."

Some common credits and deductions that can help people in the $50,000 to $300,000 range include:

- Retirement Savings Contributions Credit (Saver's Credit): If you're on the lower end of the income range and contribute to a retirement plan, you might qualify for a tax credit for doing so. This can be up to 50% of your contribution (for low incomes) and encourages retirement saving. It phases out at higher incomes, but for those who are eligible, it's a nice bonus.
- Child Tax Credit (CTC): Families with children under 17 can get a credit of up to $2,000 per qualifying child in recent years. The credit starts phasing out at relatively high-income levels (around $200k single or $400k married for full credit), so many middle and upper-middle earners still get some or all of this credit. Unlike a deduction, the CTC directly lowers your tax, and it's partially refundable (meaning if it exceeds your tax, you could get a refund). It's a significant benefit for those raising kids.

- Education Credits: If you or your dependents are in college, the United States of America Opportunity Tax Credit (up to $2,500 per student for undergrads) or Lifetime Learning Credit (up to $2,000) can reduce the cost of tuition via tax savings. These phase out in the middle-income ranges (for instance, the AOTC starts phasing out above ~$80k single/$160k married), but if you qualify, it's free money toward education expenses.
- Homeowner Deductions: Owning a home can provide deductions for mortgage interest and property taxes. Due to the higher standard deduction introduced in recent tax law, you'll need sufficient itemized deductions for these to matter (e.g., if interest plus taxes and charitable donations exceed the standard deduction). If they do, you could deduct the interest on mortgages (up to loan limits) and up to $10,000 of state/local taxes (the SALT cap). These deductions effectively subsidize home ownership by reducing the after-tax cost. For example, if you're in a 24% bracket and pay $10,000 in mortgage interest, you save $2,400 in taxes if you itemize.
- Charitable Contributions: to qualified charities are deductible if you itemize. Beyond the altruistic benefits, this can be a way to align your money with your values and get a tax benefit. Some higher earners use strategies like donor-advised funds to bunch donations in one year for a bigger deduction, then grant the money to charities over time.
- Above-the-Line Deductions: Even if you don't itemize, there are certain deductions everyone can take "above the line" (adjustments to taxable income). For instance, contributions to a Traditional IRA (if eligible), health

insurance premiums for self-employed folks, student loan interest (for those under income caps), or HSA contributions are all adjustments that reduce your adjusted gross income. Each of these can save you some tax and possibly help you qualify for other credits that have income phase-outs.

The key point is to educate yourself or get professional tax advice on which credits and deductions apply to you. Middle and upper-middle-income taxpayers often miss opportunities simply because they didn't realize they qualified.

A little planning, like bunching deductions into one year, contributing a bit more to an IRA, or timing an expense differently, can increase your tax breaks. Those tax savings can then be redirected into your savings or investments, accelerating your wealth building. Remember: any time you legally reduce your tax burden, you are effectively getting a higher return on your income.

As one financial strategist put it, the wealthy don't have secret tricks; they just make sure to "identify unnecessary tax liabilities" and use every available deduction and credit. You can do the same.

Tailored Tax Tactics: W-2 vs. Self-Employed

Everyone's tax situation is a bit different. A major factor is whether you earn income as an employee (W-2 income) or are self-employed/own a business (1099 or business income) or a mix of both. The tax strategies available to you can differ in these scenarios. We'll break down a few considerations for each.

Tax Planning for W-2 Employees (Salary and Wage Earners)

If you work as an employee receiving a W-2, your taxes are generally simpler, your employer withholds income taxes and payroll taxes from your paycheck automatically. While this makes life easier since you don't have to calculate and send quarterly tax payments, it also means you have fewer deductions.

You can't, for example, deduct your commuting costs or home office as an employee (These types of unreimbursed job expenses are no longer deductible for most). However, W-2 earners do have some great strategies at their disposal:

- Optimize your paycheck withholding: Make sure your withholding is calibrated to your actual tax liability. Too little withheld can lead to a big bill (and potentially underpayment penalties) at tax time, and too much withheld means you're giving the government an interest-free loan (you'll get a big refund, but that money could have been earning interest or reducing debt during the year). Use the IRS W-4 form and online calculators to adjust your withholdings so that you hit close to break-even at year-end. This is part of tax planning that ensures you have the right amount taken out.

- Maximize employer-sponsored benefits: We mentioned retirement plans and HSAs already. As a W-2 earner, these are often your primary tax-saving tools.

- Contribute enough to your 401(k) to get the full employer match (at minimum) and ideally work toward maxing it out if you can.

- Contributing to a traditional 401(k) can also help keep your income below certain thresholds (for example, if your household is near the limit for a Roth IRA contribution or certain credits, a 401 (k) deduction can bring your income down and preserve those benefits).

- If your employer offers a Flexible Spending Account (FSA) for healthcare or dependent care, consider using those as well. They let you pay certain expenses with pre-tax dollars (though they have a "use it or lose it" rule each year).

- An FSA for childcare (dependent care FSA) can be especially valuable for working parents, allowing up to $5,000 of tax-free contributions for childcare expenses.

- Leverage payroll deductions: Beyond retirement and health accounts, some employers let you deduct things like transit passes or parking fees pre-tax. While these are smaller tax savings, they do add up. For example, $100 per month of pre-tax transit benefits might save ~$300 in taxes over a year if you're in a ~25% combined tax bracket. The general principle is: if your employer offers any pre-tax benefit, use it rather than paying those expenses with after-tax dollars.

- Standard vs. itemized deduction planning: If you own a home or have significant deductible expenses, plan your itemized deductions. If your itemized total (mortgage interest, property taxes, charitable gifts, etc.) is just at the cusp of exceeding the standard deduction, consider "bunching" certain expenses in one year.

- You might make two years' worth of charitable donations in one calendar year, or schedule elective medical procedures in the same year, to get over the standard deduction threshold and maximize your tax benefit. In alternate years, take the standard deduction. This way, over a multi-year period, you net more deductions than if you kept them split. W-2 earners can use this timing strategy since their income is relatively steady and the deductions are often in their control to time.

- Use tax software or a professional to double-check: Tax planning for employees isn't extremely complex, but it's easy to overlook something. Using good tax software or consulting a tax professional can help identify deductions or credits you might be missing.

For instance, if you went back to school part-time, you could get an education credit, or if you moved for a new job, certain moving expenses for the military, etc.). They can also help ensure your withholding is correct. It's worth the small effort; any refund you get because you discovered a missed deduction is effectively extra money in your pocket from good planning.

Overall, W-2 employees should focus on the "big wins": retirement accounts, HSAs/FSAs, and making sure to grab every credit or adjustment (like student loan interest) available. While you can't write off a home office or many work expenses, you also don't have to pay self-employment tax directly (more on that next) since your employer covers half of your Social Security/Medicare taxes. Use the simplicity of your situation to your advantage by automating your tax-saving contributions and consistently investing those tax savings. A dollar saved on tax is a dollar you can invest for yourself.

Tax Planning for Self-Employed Individuals (Freelancers, Contractors, and Business Owners)

If you're self-employed whether running your own business, freelancing, or doing gig work you enter a more complex but potentially more rewarding arena of tax planning.

The U.S. tax code provides many deductions and strategies for business owners that are not available to employees, as a reward for entrepreneurship and the risks business owners take. However, along with those opportunities comes additional responsibility: you have to handle tax withholding and compliance yourself. Here are key tax considerations and strategies for the self-employed:

Plan for Self-Employment Tax: When you work for yourself, you must pay self-employment (SE) tax, which is essentially the Social Security and Medicare tax that an employer would normally split with you. The SE tax rate is 15.3% (12.4% Social Security + 2.9% Medicare) on your net self-employment income. As a self-employed person, you pay both the employee and employer halves of these taxes. This means, compared to a W-2 worker, you're paying about double in FICA taxes on the same amount of earnings. It's critical to account for this in your budget and pricing.

The good news: when you file your tax return, you get to deduct half of your self-employment tax as an above-the-line deduction (since the "employer half" is considered a business expense). But you still have to pay it throughout the year. Set aside money (roughly 25-30% of your profits, or more if you're a high-income earner) for taxes so you're not caught short. Pay quarterly estimated taxes to the IRS and state to avoid penalties because no one is withholding taxes from your payments except you. Staying disciplined on this tax requirement prevents a nasty surprise at tax time.

Business Expense Deductions; Know Them, Track Them: One huge advantage of being self-employed is that you can deduct ordinary and necessary expenses of earning your income on your Schedule C (or business return). These expenses directly reduce your taxable profit, lowering both income tax and self-employment tax.

Some valuable write-offs that employees cannot take but you, as a business owner, can include:

- The Home Office Deduction (if you use a portion of your home exclusively for business, you can deduct a portion of your rent/mortgage, utilities, insurance, etc. based on square footage)
- Vehicle expenses for business use (you can deduct a standard mileage rate, e.g., 70 cents per mile in 2025 for business miles driven, which often covers gas, maintenance, depreciation implicitly, or you can deduct actual expenses proportional to business use)
- A portion of your phone and internet bills if used for business
- Equipment and supplies
- Travel for business purposes (be sure to document!)
- Meals with clients (50% deductible in many cases)
- Professional services and education related to the business
- Business insurance and licensing costs

Essentially, most of the money you spend to operate or grow your business likely has some deductibility. Keep detailed records and save receipts to substantiate your business expenses. Every dollar of expense you write off is a dollar not taxed.

Many small business owners drastically reduce their taxable income (on paper) by wisely and legitimately deducting all their business costs, sometimes to the point where their effective tax rate becomes very low. As one CPA noted, "operating your own business introduces many potential tax deductions not accessible as a W-2 employee."

If you own a business, you don't want to leave these on the table, so learn the rules or work with a tax advisor who can identify them.

- Retirement plans for the self-employed: Another major opportunity is setting up your own self-employed retirement plan. Whereas a regular employee is limited to a 401(k) from their employer, you can establish plans like a SEP-IRA, Solo 401(k), SIMPLE IRA, or even a Defined Benefit pension plan for your business. These allow much higher contribution limits in many cases. For example, a SEP-IRA allows you to contribute up to ~20% of your net self-employment income (with a max of $69,000 for 2025). A Solo 401(k) allows a combination of employee deferral (up to $22,500) plus an employer profit-sharing contribution (up to the same effective maximum of around $69,000 between both). If you have a high-earning freelance gig or small business, you could potentially shelter tens of thousands of dollars per year pre-tax in these plans, far exceeding the normal IRA limits. This lowers your taxable income now, potentially saving a huge chunk in taxes and rapidly building your retirement investments. It's not unusual for a successful self-employed person to "zero out" their federal income tax bill by maxing out a retirement plan alongside other deductions. For instance, contributing $50,000 to a solo 401(k) as a 55-year-old not only supercharges your retirement, but if you're in the 24% tax bracket, it saves about $12,000 in taxes right off the bat. It "keeps funds out of the IRS's hands now and delivers them down the road when you withdraw in retirement". In short, being self-employed lets you play by a special set of retirement rules use them to your advantage.

- Business structure and tax status: Depending on your income level and business type, you may benefit from choosing a specific business entity for tax purposes. Many solo entrepreneurs start as a sole proprietor or single-member LLC, which is simple, and all income is taxed on your Schedule C. As profits grow, some switch to an S-Corporation status. An S-Corp is a pass-through entity like an LLC, but it allows you to split your income into two parts: a "reasonable salary" (which is subject to payroll taxes) and the rest as a distribution of profits (which is not subject to self-employment tax). By doing this, an S-Corp can save on the SE tax because the dividend portion avoids the 15.3% tax. For example, if your business makes $200,000 and you pay yourself a salary of $120,000 (reasonable for your role) and take $80,000 as distribution, that $80k avoids the 15.3% tax, potentially saving about $12,000 in taxes. There is additional paperwork and fees (including payroll service costs) with an S-Corp, so it usually makes sense once your net income is beyond a certain point (many CPAs suggest it's worth considering above $50,000 to $100,000 of profit). Consult a tax advisor to see if this strategy fits your situation. The tax savings can be significant, but you must follow IRS rules carefully. The Brighton Jones CPA team explains that an S-Corp "allows you to take some income as non-self-employment earnings" (thus reducing SE tax), which is exactly the benefit we're discussing. Choosing the right business entity is part of tax planning for self-employed people and can be a powerful savings lever.

- Qualified Business Income (QBI) deduction: Currently, small business owners (sole props, LLCs, S-Corps, etc.) may be eligible for the QBI deduction; up to 20% of your business profit can be deducted after all the above, as a special tax break. There are limitations and phase-outs for higher incomes and certain service professions, but many in the mid-income range qualify, especially if married with a total taxable income under around $364,000 (2024). For example, if your consulting business earns $100k net, you might get a $20k deduction off that due to QBI, cutting your taxable income further. In one real tax planning case, a business owner's strategy made him eligible for the 20% QBI deduction, contributing to an overall $95,000 reduction in tax liability for that year. The QBI deduction was enacted in 2018 as an incentive for small businesses; with 2025 tax reforms it's in effect for now. Keep it on your radar and ask your tax professional about it. Sometimes a tactic like lowering your taxable income (through a retirement plan contribution, for instance) can enable a larger QBI deduction if you're near a phase-out threshold.

- Stay organized and seek professional help: Taxes for the self-employed can get complex quickly. It pays to keep good books (consider using accounting software or a professional) and perhaps hire a CPA or tax advisor who specializes in small businesses. They can help you implement all the above strategies (and ensure you don't miss any).

- Your goal should not just be compliance

Remember, starting a business doesn't just create additional income; it provides a way to take control of taxes and keep more of your money working for you. Tax planning is where you exercise that control.

Real-Life Examples of Tax Planning Success

To see how these strategies translate into real-world results, let's look at a few relatable stories of individuals who used tax planning to build wealth. These examples cover a range from modest incomes to high earners (all within the $50,000 - $300,000 bracket) and illustrate how smart tax moves can make a big difference:

The Early-Career Saver: Meet Sarah, age 27, a software developer earning $70,000 (W-2 employee). When she got her first job, she decided to contribute 10% of her salary ($7,000) to her 401(k). Not only did her company match a portion of that (free money!), but her taxable income dropped to $63,000. This move saved her roughly $1,500 in federal taxes for the year (she's in the 22% bracket).

Sarah used part of her tax refund to pay off student loans and invested the rest in a Roth IRA. Every year, she increases her 401(k) contribution a bit and maxes her Roth IRA. After five years, she's built over $75,000 in retirement investments between her 401(k) and Roth a nest egg that is growing tax advantaged. By starting early, Sarah also locked in decades of compounding. The tax planning here was simple automate retirement contributions but it has put her significantly ahead of her peers in net worth.

She notes that she doesn't miss the money coming out of her paycheck, because she never saw it to begin with. And knowing she's saving on taxes makes it even easier to stick with the plan. Sarah is on track to achieve financial independence well before traditional retirement age, thanks in part to the discipline of tax-efficient saving in her 20s.

The Freelancer's Turnaround: Jordan is a 35-year-old freelance graphic designer who made about $120,000 in gross income last year from various clients. In his first year of full-time freelancing, Jordan treated all his earnings like take-home pay and got hit with a massive tax bill the next April. He hadn't realized he needed to set aside money for taxes throughout the year, and he hadn't tracked his business expenses well.

After a stressful scramble to pay what he owed, Jordan got serious about tax planning. He opened a separate business bank account and started paying quarterly estimated taxes. He also educated himself on deductions: he now diligently logs his work mileage, home office dimensions, receipts for software subscriptions, new computer equipment, and even part of his internet and phone bills.

Come tax time, these legitimate business expenses added up to $30,000, bringing his taxable profit down to $90,000. Furthermore, he opened a Solo 401(k) and contributed $20,000 to it, cutting his taxable income to $70,000.

Between deducting half his self-employment tax and claiming the QBI deduction, Jordan's overall taxable income fell to about $50,000 similar to what a salaried person making $60k might have. The result: his federal tax due dropped dramatically.

In fact, Jordan saved over $15,000 in taxes compared to the prior year, all by using tax planning strategies available to the self-employed. That $15,000 stayed in his business and personal investment accounts rather than going to Uncle Sam. He used part of the savings to upgrade his equipment (further improving his business) and invested the rest in an index fund.

Jordan's story shows how quickly a self-employed person can turn taxes from a burden into a wealth-building ally. By taking control of his tax situation, he not only reduced stress but also effectively boosted his take-home profit, which he's now using to secure his financial future.

The High Earner "Not Rich Yet" Couple: Alex and Maria, in their early 40s, are a dual-income couple earning $280,000 combined, in high cost of living California. Despite the high income, they felt like they weren't building wealth commensurate with their earnings (a classic "HENRY" High Earner, Not Rich Yet scenario). They decided to optimize their finances, and a big part of that was tax planning.

A Tax Plan to Generate Wealth

First, they maximized both of their 401(k) contributions (deferring $22,500 each per year pre-tax). This move alone shielded $45,000 of their income from immediate taxation. At roughly a 32% combined federal/state marginal tax rate, that saved them about $14,000 in taxes in one year. They also put $7,750 into an HSA (family max), saving about $2,500 in taxes on that contribution, and started investing the HSA money for long-term growth.

Next, since their income is too high for direct Roth IRA contributions, they each performed a Backdoor Roth IRA, contributing $6,500 to a traditional IRA and then immediately converted it to Roth. Over the years, doing this annually will quietly build a sizable pot of tax-free money for them; even a single $6,500 Roth contribution can grow to around $35,000 over 25 years, so they know this strategy will likely add tens of thousands of tax-free dollars to their retirement.

Additionally, Alex and Maria have two young kids. They take advantage of the Child Tax Credit (phased out partially at their income, but still a few hundred dollars benefit) and contribute to a 529 college savings plan for the kids (no federal deduction, but their state gives a small tax break for it).

Lastly, they met with a CPA who advised them on charitable giving. They bundled donations using a donor-advised fund, allowing them to itemize in one year (and exceed the SALT cap impact), then take the standard deduction the next. This tactic saved them an extra $2,000 in taxes every two-year cycle compared to their old method of donating smaller amounts annually.

Altogether, these strategies mean that each year Alex and Maria are keeping roughly $20,000 more of their money after tax than they would have otherwise.

Rather than lifestyle-creeping that money away, they now purposefully channel it into extra mortgage payments and a taxable investment account. In just five years of this plan, their net worth has jumped considerably: they've paid off all remaining student debts, built a six-figure brokerage account, and are on track to retire comfortably in their 60s.

This couple's story underlines that even if you earn a lot, you won't build wealth unless you actively keep a lot of what you earn. By aggressively leveraging tax-advantaged options, they turned a high income into real, growing wealth, proving that tax planning isn't just for the ultra-rich; it's for anyone who wants to get ahead.

These stories show that proper tax planning can make a tangible difference, no matter your income level. Whether it's a young professional starting out, a self-employed individual hustling on their own terms, or a high earner optimizing in the peak career years, tax-savvy decisions translate to more money in your pocket and more capital growing for your future. The strategies used above from 401(k)s to HSAs to business deductions are readily available to most people in the U.S. with a bit of research or professional guidance.

The Power of Tax Planning: Keeping More of What You Earn

Taxes are often seen as an inevitable burden, but with knowledge and planning, they can be managed and minimized to help you reach your financial goals faster. The key takeaways from this chapter are simple: Integrate tax considerations into your financial decisions year-round.

Don't wait until April to think about taxes; by then, the best you can do is record history. Instead, plan in advance:

- Contribute to those retirement and HSA accounts
- Track your expenses
- Adjust your withholdings,
- Look for opportunities that fit your situation.

The U.S. tax system, complex as it may be, actually offers a roadmap to financial opportunities, guiding you toward behaviors (like saving and investing) that ultimately benefit you. The cumulative effect of consistently doing this can be life-changing when you learn how to do it effectively.

Remember, the goal of tax planning is not to cheat the system, but to make sure you're not overpaying. Every dollar saved in taxes (legally) is a dollar that can earn investment returns, fund your dreams, or build your legacy. Over time, those dollars become hundreds, then thousands, then hundreds of thousands.

By recognizing that taxes play a central role in personal finance and by treating tax planning as an essential component of your wealth-building strategy, you empower yourself to keep more of what you earn. In personal finance, it's often said that it's not about how much you make, it's about how much you keep, and taxes are usually the single biggest factor in that equation.

Take control: use the strategies in this chapter, consult professionals if needed, and make a plan to pay less to Uncle Sam and more to yourself. You will thank yourself when you have the opportunity to enjoy your future wealth

CHAPTER EIGHT: RISK MANAGEMENT

When I first arrived in the United States, I had never heard of things like renters' insurance, deductibles, or a health savings account. I quickly realized that life in the United States of America comes with a lot of "what ifs."

What if I get sick?

What if my car gets totaled?

What if I pass away unexpectedly?

These questions can become paralyzing unless you understand how to manage risk wisely.

In my personal finance journey, I've adopted one core belief about insurance: **You only manage risks you cannot bear.** This simple philosophy has helped me and many others avoid financial disasters and protect what matters most.

Understanding Risk in Personal Finance

Risk is a part of life. Every time you get behind the wheel, take a flight, walk into a hospital, or start a business, you expose yourself to risk. Most risks are small and manageable out-of-pocket. But some risks like a major medical emergency, a house fire, or an untimely death can completely derail your financial life. That's where insurance comes in. Insurance allows you to transfer

financial risks you can't handle yourself to an insurance company.

In exchange for a premium, the insurer bears those catastrophic risks so you don't have to. However, not all insurance is created equal, and not every possible risk is worth insuring. The key is to ensure against the big risks that you truly cannot bear on your own, and not waste money over-insuring against minor issues.

Health Insurance: Protecting Against the Unexpected

A medical emergency can bankrupt a family. In the United States of America, where the cost of a single hospital visit or surgery can run into the tens of thousands, health insurance is

Real-Life Example: A friend of mine once skipped health insurance to "save money." A few months later, he was rushed to the ER for a ruptured appendix. He survived, but the $35,000 hospital bill nearly ruined him financially. (For context, one uninsured patient in Colorado was billed $35,906 for an emergency appendectomy.) It took my friend over five years to pay off the debt.

Lesson: If you can't afford a major surgery out of pocket, you can't afford to go without health insurance. Unfortunately, stories like his are common; medical issues contribute to about 62% of personal bankruptcies in the U.S. Health insurance exists to prevent a sudden illness or accident from turning into a financial catastrophe.

Life Insurance: Creating Security for Those You Love

Life insurance isn't for you; it's for the people you leave behind. If you have dependents or financial obligations, life insurance ensures your family won't suffer financially if something happens to you. It provides a tax-free cash payout (the **death benefit**) to your beneficiaries, offering them a vital safety net.

Despite its importance, roughly half of the United States of America's citizens have no life insurance coverage, even though about two-thirds say they worry about their family's financial well-being if the primary earner dies.

Real-Life Example: A single mother I worked with had two young children and a modest income. She bought a $250,000 term life insurance policy for about $28 per month. When she passed away unexpectedly from a health condition, that policy payout allowed her sister to raise the children without financial struggle. It became the foundation of a stable life for them, covering their living expenses and future education.

Lesson: Term life insurance is inexpensive and can be life-changing for those you love. In fact, a healthy 20 40-year-old can typically get a $250,000 term policy for around $24 to $29 per month. For the price of a family dinner each month, you can create security for your loved ones. Life insurance isn't about betting on your life; it's about providing peace of mind that if the worst happens, your family is protected.

Property & Auto Insurance: Guarding Your Assets

Your car, your home, and even your phone are assets that all carry the risk of loss or damage. For autos, basic liability insurance is required in almost every state if you drive. If you lease or finance a car, **full coverage** (which includes collision and comprehensive) is usually required by the lender. If you own a home (or have a mortgage), homeowners' insurance is mandatory to protect the structure. But beyond legal requirements, you should make sure your coverage truly protects your finances in the event of a **total**

loss. Don't just buy the minimum to satisfy the law or the bank; consider the worst-case scenarios.

For example, a house fire could cause devastating losses, and the **average** homeowner's insurance claim for fire damage is over **$83,000**. Without adequate insurance, an event like that could wipe out your savings or even bankrupt you. Similarly, auto accidents can be incredibly costly. In 2023, the **average** auto liability claim for bodily injury was about **$26,500** (and about $6,500 for property damage) If you only carry state-minimum auto insurance, an accident you cause could leave you personally on the hook for amounts above your coverage limits.

Tip: Make sure your coverage is high enough to cover a total loss of your property and to shield you from major liability. This might include replacement-cost coverage on your home, and higher liability limits on your car (many experts recommend at least 100/300/100 or even $250k+ liability coverage on auto policies). If you have a car loan, consider **GAP insurance** (Guaranteed Asset Protection). This covers the "gap" between what your auto insurer pays if your car is totaled and what you still owe on the loan.

Example: Years ago, when my vehicle was repossessed after an accident and loan default, I didn't just lose the car; I lost my personal stability. I was still stuck with debt for a car I no longer had. Later, as I rebuilt my financial life, I understood that proper insurance (including collision coverage and GAP coverage on a financed car) could have helped prevent that setback. Don't let one misfortune cascade into a financial spiral.

Business Insurance: Protecting Your Dreams

If you run a business, you're carrying significant financial risk every day. Whether it's liability for your services, coverage for your inventory and equipment, or protection from employee and customer claims, insurance is your financial shield for your business dreams. One lawsuit or disaster can be enough to shut your doors if you're not insured.

Real-Life Example: When I acquired my first retail store, I naïvely didn't fully understand business insurance. I was focused on growing sales and managing expenses, and insurance felt like just another cost. But I quickly learned that even a small accident like a customer slipping on a wet floor could result in a costly lawsuit. (For instance, the average **slip-and-fall** injury claim against a business is around **$20,000**, and if a lawsuit is involved, a general liability claim can average more than **$75,000** to defend and settle.)

I immediately purchased a simple general liability policy, along with property insurance for my inventory. That coverage gave me peace of mind and literally kept me in business when an incident eventually happened (a minor store mishap that led to an insurance claim).

Lesson: Business insurance isn't just about protection; it's a tool for **sustainability and credibility**. It shows you're serious about honoring your obligations if something goes wrong, and it ensures a single unexpected event won't derail years of hard work.

Avoiding the Trap of Over-Insurance

Insurance is **protection**, not an investment or a profit-making tool. One common mistake is over-insuring or buying policies you don't really need. Some insurance agents (or companies) may try to sell you coverage that sounds good but isn't cost-effective for your situation. Remember: every dollar spent on insurance should be protecting a risk you truly cannot bear alone. You don't need insurance for every minor inconvenience or highly unlikely event. Insuring everything is a good way to bleed your budget for little benefit. In fact, many potential "Catastrophes" in life are **not worth insuring against at** all.

For example, expensive extended warranties or niche policies often have low payout relative to their cost. As the folks at Ramsey Solutions put it, the purpose of insurance is to shield you from large losses, not to cover small expenses or serve as a savings plan. If an adverse event wouldn't financially devastate you, you're usually better off self-insuring (i.e., building an emergency fund) for that risk instead of paying an insurer. Don't fall for insurance gimmicks and add-ons that aren't truly necessary.

When evaluating any insurance, ask yourself a few key questions:

Can I afford to cover this risk out-of-pocket? (If a loss happened, could you comfortably pay for it from savings or income?)

What is the realistic likelihood of this risk occurring? (High-frequency risks might be better managed through savings; low-frequency but high-cost risks are the ones to insure.)

Is there a more affordable way to manage this risk? (Could you mitigate it through behavior, maintenance, or cheaper coverage?)

If the answer to the first question is "no", it means a loss would be more than you could handle alone. It's a strong sign that insurance is needed. If you can handle it, or the likelihood is extremely low, you might skip or reduce that coverage. Essentially, **don't over-insure**. By avoiding unnecessary policies, you free up money that can be saved or invested elsewhere.

My Personal Checklist for Insurance Planning

Over the years, I've developed a simple checklist to ensure I'm only managing the risks I cannot bear myself. I review this list periodically to make sure I have the right protections in place:

Health: Do I have major medical coverage in place for myself and my family? (Medical bills can pile up fast and devastate finances without insurance.)

Life: If others rely on my income, do I have an adequate term life insurance policy to provide for them if I'm gone?

Auto: Is my auto insurance coverage sufficient for a total loss and for liability if I cause a serious accident? (Think about replacing your vehicle and covering injuries/damages to others.)

Home/Renters: Am I protected from fire, theft, or liability at my residence? (Even renters need insurance for their belongings and liability. Your landlord's policy won't cover your stuff or negligence.)

Business: If I own a business or side hustle, are my business activities properly insured for liability and property loss?

Disability: What happens if I can't work for an extended period due to injury or illness? Do I have disability insurance or sufficient savings? (About 1 in 4 of today's 20-year-olds will experience a disabling condition before retirement age, so this is a real risk to consider.)

Umbrella Policy: Do I have significant assets that exceed my basic liability coverage limits? (If your net worth is higher than your auto/home liability limits, an umbrella policy can provide an extra layer of protection.

This checklist serves as a quick personal audit of risk management. For each item, I aim to answer **"Yes, I'm covered"** because these are the areas where a lack of coverage could truly bankrupt me or my family. By saying "yes" to only the insurance that matters, I'm effectively saying "no" to unnecessary worry about life's big "what ifs." In your own life, make sure you have a plan for the risks you can't bear, and don't sweat the rest. With wise insurance choices and a solid emergency fund, you can face the future confidently, knowing you've managed the risks that matter most.

In summary, **only manage (insure) the risks you cannot handle over the short-term**. That way, you'll protect yourself from financial devastation while avoiding the trap of overpaying for needless coverage. It's a balanced approach that brings peace of mind and keeps your financial plan on track, no matter what life throws your way.

CONCLUSION

Redefining Financial Freedom

Most people think financial freedom means paying off all debt. While debt reduction is wise, I believe that's only part of the story. Financial independence is when your essential bills are fully covered by residual income money that flows in without you working for it daily.

For example, imagine two people:

Person A: Debt-free, no mortgage, no credit cards, but must work full-time to pay for food, healthcare, utilities, and transportation. If they stop working, their bills will quickly pile up.

Person B: Has a mortgage but owns a rental property that pays the mortgage plus covers groceries and utilities. Even with debt, Person B can survive without working for months or even years because income keeps flowing.

Which person is truly free? Person B.

Why Debt-Free Isn't Always Freedom

Being debt-free is often celebrated as the ultimate goal. But freedom isn't about what you owe it's about what you own that pays you back.

Imagine someone pays off their car loan. That's great, but the car doesn't generate money.

Compare that with someone who still has a small loan on a duplex rental property. Even after paying the loan, they earn $500 per month in cash flow. That $500 helps cover food, gas, or utilities without them clocking in at work.

True freedom is measured in cash flow, not just debt balance.

The Residual Income Principle

Residual income comes in many shapes. Here are some practical forms:

Investments: Buying shares in companies that pay dividends. Example: If you own $10,000 in dividend stocks paying 4%, that's $400 every year enough to cover a utility bill without lifting a finger.

Rental Properties: A two-bedroom apartment that generates $300 after the mortgage and expenses. That could permanently cover your grocery bill.

Businesses: An online course or digital product you create once and keep selling. A friend of mine sells a $50 eBook on Amazon. Even if he sells just 20 copies a month, that's $1,000 income without extra work.

Royalties/Creative Work: If you write music, books, or software, you can receive payments long after the initial work is done. For instance, a local pastor I know published a devotional book. Years later, the royalties still pay his cell phone bill. The power of residual income is that it compounds you can add multiple streams until they cover all your essentials.

Building Residual Income to Cover Essentials

The strategy is simple: Start with your core monthly bills. Let's use an example:

- Rent/Mortgage: $1,000
- Utilities: $300
- Groceries: $500
- Transportation: $200
- Insurance: $200

Total Essentials = $2,200 per month

Now, your mission is to build enough residual income to cover $2,200.

- A rental property generating $700
- A part-time online business producing $800
- Stock dividends giving $200
- A YouTube channel monetized for $500

That's $2,200 your essentials covered. You may still choose to work, but you'll do it by choice, not obligation.

My Journey to Residual Income

When I first came to the U.S., I thought working harder was the answer. But even with long hours, I was always one emergency away from financial crisis. My turning point was realizing I needed income that did not depend on my time.

For example, when I started Tri-City Business Services, I was trading hours for money meet clients, file taxes, do payroll. But as the business grew, I trained staff, automated systems, and added services that run whether I am present or not. Now, some revenue streams continue even if I step away. That shift from working in the business to building systems changed everything.

The True Test of Financial Independence

Here's a simple test:

If you stopped working today, how long would your income continue to cover your life?

If your answer is "until my savings run out", you are not financially independent.

If your answer is "indefinitely, because my systems keep paying", then you have achieved independence.

Example:

A teacher with no debt but only one paycheck = Not financially free.

A rideshare driver who owns two rental properties generating $1,500/month = Closer to financial freedom, even if they still drive part-time.

Closing Reflection

The key to financial independence is not about cutting every debt or working harder. It is about building income systems that pay for your essentials month after month, whether you work or not.

Freedom is when your **residual income > essential expenses.**

At that point, you're no longer working to survive you're working to thrive.

The 3-Step Path to Residual Income and Financial Independence

Step 1: Know Your Essentials

Write down your core monthly bills: housing, utilities, groceries, insurance, and transportation.

Example: If your essentials total $2,200 per month, that's your financial independence number.

Freedom begins with clarity know exactly what you need covered.

Step 2: Build Your First Residual Stream

Pick one area to start. Don't wait for the "perfect" one begin small and scale.

Examples: Buy a dividend-paying stock fund that gives you $30 $50 a month.

Start an online business that sells one product or service automatically.

Rent out a spare bedroom for $500 per month.

Your goal: Cover one essential bill (e.g., groceries or utilities) with residual income.

Celebrate small wins the first bill you no longer pay out of pocket is proof of progress.

Step 3: Multiply Until Covered

Keep adding streams until your essentials are fully paid by residual income.

Example:

- Rental property covers $700 (housing).
- Online store covers $400 (groceries).
- Dividend income covers $150 (utilities).
- Side business covers $950 (insurance + transportation).

Now, your $2,200 monthly essentials are covered.

At this stage, your paycheck becomes optional. Work becomes a choice, not a burden.

The Journey from Financial Fear to Financial Peace is within Your Reach

When I first arrived in the United States, I carried more than just a suitcase I carried a dream. A dream of freedom, of opportunity, of building something lasting, not just for myself, but for my family and for the generations to come. I believed that if I worked hard, kept my head down, and followed the rules (without actually knowing them!), success would follow.

What I didn't realize then was that the path to financial stability isn't just paved with effort it's paved with understanding, discipline, and sometimes, painful lessons.

My early years in the United States were marked by struggle. My wide-eyed optimism was so misplaced and did not serve me well, given the realities of starting over in a new country…and entering into a financial system I had no idea how to navigate. I was proud of my decision to come to the United States, but I was also overwhelmed. The cost of living, the complexity of the financial system, and, later, the pressure to provide for my family weighed heavily on me as they may be weighing on you now.

The United States of America's financial system and economy are, sadly, often a source of great mystery and immense money problems for those who do not know how it works.

Credit truly is everywhere offered at checkout counters, mailed to homes, even pitched as a way to "build your score." For people who don't fully understand how it works, dipping into credit you can't afford can be devastating. As I shared in these pages, I have made some life-altering mistakes. I borrowed too much, paid too little, and missed payments when cash flow was tight. Before I knew it, my credit score had plummeted, and with it, my confidence.

But more than anything, I felt stuck.

That moment became a turning point and if you are feeling stuck, or you want to avoid problems before they begin, then know that it is 100% possible to learn everything you need to know to build a strong financial foundation and future, simply by following the Basic Financial Framework that I have laid out here, the same one we use with our clients every day at Tri-City Business Services.

I hope that by reading about my story and the strategies I have shared that you realize that financial stability isn't just about getting out of debt it's about building wealth. And to do that, your mindset should shift from scarcity to stewardship of your current and future wealth.

My painful path to financial stability opened both my eyes to how uneducated most of us are when it comes to starting out in the United States of America's financial system, whether we are immigrants or we are new graduates, or business owners. This is why once I understood the mechanics of money in this country and I applied them strategically to my own life, I developed a passion to help others do the same, too.

This is what led me to start Tri-City Business Services.

I didn't want to build just another accounting firm. I wanted to create a place where people could come not just for tax prep or investment advice, but for guidance, education, and empowerment. I wanted to help others avoid the mistakes I made and recover from the ones they couldn't. I wanted to serve immigrants, small business owners, young professionals, and families who felt overwhelmed by the financial system and didn't know where to start. At Tri-City Business Services, we don't just crunch numbers. We listen. We teach. We walk alongside our clients as they navigate life's financial decisions from buying a home to starting a business to planning for retirement. We believe that everyone deserves access to sound advice and that financial literacy is the foundation of freedom.

Looking back, I'm grateful for every setback. Because each one taught me something, I now use to help others. I've seen firsthand how money mistakes can derail dreams but I've also seen how they can be reversed. With the right mindset, the right knowledge and tools, and the right support, anyone can turn their financial life around.

If you're reading this and feeling discouraged, I want you to know, you're not alone.

Money mistakes are common. They're part of the learning curve. But they're also avoidable and this book was written to help you do just that. I've shared my story to encourage you. To show you that even when things feel hopeless, there is a way forward.

And if you've already made mistakes, know this: they are reversible.

You can rebuild your credit. You can pay off your debt. You can learn to invest, to save, to plan. You can create a life of financial stability and peace not just for yourself, but for your family and your community.

I truly believe that financial freedom isn't reserved for the wealthy it's available to anyone willing to learn, to act, and to believe.

If you need help, reach out to us at Tri-City Business Services. We will help you succeed.

APPENDIX

Investment Reference Sheet

1. Saving vs. Investing (Quick Overview)

Category	Saving	Investing
Purpose	Preserve money	Grow money
Typical Return	0.5–2%	5–10% (long-term avg.)
Risk Level	Very low	Moderate to high
Access to Funds	Easy (liquid)	Limited (best for long-term)
Examples	Savings accounts, CDs	Stocks, ETFs, bonds, real estate

2. Investment Scenarios: $100 per Month at 7% Growth

Investor	Start Age	End Age	Years of Investment	Total Invested	Final Value at 65 (Approx.)
Person A	20	65	45 years	$54,000	$319,000
Person B	30	65	35 years	$42,000	$168,000
Person C	40	65	25 years	$30,000	$83,000

3. Top Growth Stocks (10–20 Year Annualized Returns)

Stock	Sector	Avg. Annual Return	Notes
Apple (AAPL)	Technology	26%	Driven by iPhone ecosystem & services growth.
Microsoft (MSFT)	Technology	22%	Cloud expansion & steady dividends.
Nvidia (NVDA)	Semiconductors	45%	AI & GPU dominance; rapid compounding.
Amazon (AMZN)	E-Commerce	25%	AWS and retail reinvestment growth.
Alphabet (GOOGL)	Technology	20%	Advertising and AI diversification

4. Top Growth ETFs (10–20 Year Annualized Returns)

ETF	Description	Avg. Annual Return (Approx.)
QQQ (Invesco QQQ)	Nasdaq-100 index; tech-heavy fund	16%
VUG (Vanguard Growth ETF)	Large-cap U.S. growth exposure	13%
IWF (iShares Russell 1000 Growth ETF)	Large/mid-cap growth index	12%
SMH (VanEck Semiconductor ETF)	Semiconductor industry focus	28%
SOXX (iShares Semiconductor ETF)	Broad semiconductor exposure	25%

5. Best Investment Platforms

Platform	Key Features
Fidelity	No trading fees, fractional shares, strong tools
Charles Schwab	Commission-free trades, excellent research
Vanguard	Low-cost index & retirement funds
TD Ameritrade	Great education & research tools
M1 Finance	Automated investing with fractional shares

6. Automated Investing Platforms (Robo-Advisors)

Platform	Key Features	Annual Fee	Ideal For
Betterment	Goal-based investing, auto rebalancing	0.25%	Beginners
Wealthfront	Tax-loss harvesting, smart portfolios	0.25%	Tech-savvy investors
SoFi Invest	$0 fees, free coaching	0%	New investors
Ellevest	Gender-focused investing, education tools	0.25–0.50%	Women professionals
Schwab Intelligent Portfolios	No advisory fee, auto rebalancing	0%	Balanced portfolios

7. The Power of Time and Rate in Investing

You invest $100 per month. No tricks, no windfalls, just consistent saving and the growth of compound interest.

Years of Investing	Return (7%)	Return (8%)	Return (10%)	Total Invested
20 years	$52,000	$57,000	$69,000	$24,000
30 years	$123,000	$136,000	$197,000	$36,000
40 years	$240,000	$293,000	$556,000	$48,000

What This Shows:

The same $100 grows very differently depending on time and rate. Staying invested longer can turn thousands into hundreds of thousands. A 3% increase in return over 40 years nearly doubles your outcome.

The best investors aren't those who time the market—they're those who stay in it.

8. Example: Early vs Late Investor ($100/month, 7% Growth)

Investor	Contribution Period	Total Invested	Final Value at 65 (Approx.)
Person A	Age 20–30 (10 yrs, then stops)	$12,000	$177,000
Person B	Age 30–65 (35 yrs continuous)	$42,000	$166,000

Key Takeaway: The earlier you start investing, the greater the impact of compounding. Investing is not gambling - it's a disciplined act of stewardship.

Understanding the Credit System

Credit Score Ratings and Real-World Scenarios

Credit Score Ranges and Ratings

Credit Score Range	Rating
800–850	Excellent
740–799	Very Good
670–739	Good
580–669	Fair
300–579	Poor (Bad Credit)

Buying a $20,000 Car with a 5-Year Loan

Person	Credit Score Range	Interest Rate	Monthly Payment	Total Interest
A	750 (Very Good)	4%	$368	$2,100
B	600 (Poor)	12%	$445	$6,700

Buying a $300,000 Home with a 30-Year Mortgage

Person	Credit Score Range	Interest Rate	Monthly Payment	Total Interest
A	760 (Very Good)	6.5%	$1,896	$382,500
B	620 (Poor)	8.5%	$2,301	$528,300

Paying Off $40,000 in Student Loans (10-Year Term)

Credit Quality	Interest Rate	Monthly Payment	Total Interest
Good (670–739)	5.5%	$435	$12,200
Poor (300–579)	9%	$507	$20,800

Buying $5,000 in Furniture (3-Year Store Credit Plan)

Credit Quality	Interest Rate	Monthly Payment	Total Cost
Good (670–739)	0–5%	$150	$5,200
Poor (300–579)	20%	$186	$6,700

Renting an Apartment

Credit Quality	Outcome
Good (670–739)	Easy approval, low deposit, access to better units
Poor (300–579)	High deposit (1–2 months' rent), may need co-signer or be denied

Credit Usage

Month	Spending Decision	Balance	Credit Limit	Utilization %	Score Impact	New Score
1	Buy $200 in groceries and pay in full	$0	$1,000	0%	+10	690
2	Charge $500 and carry a balance	$500	$1,000	50%	-10	680
3	Pay off $300, balance now $200	$200	$1,000	20%	+5	685
4	Max out card with emergency repair ($1,000)	$1,000	$1,000	100%	-40	645
5	Pay down to $200	$200	$1,000	20%	+10	655

⇒Learning Points

- Ideal credit usage is below 30% of available credit.
- Maxing out cards damages scores.
- Paying off balances fully helps build and maintain strong credit.
- Consistent responsible usage can repair damage over time.

Loan Payment Simulation

Month	Loan Balance	Payment Made?	Late/On Time	Score Impact	New Score
1	$5,000	$200	On Time	+10	690
2	$4,800	$0	Missed	-40	650
3	$4,800	$200	On Time	+5	655
4	$4,600	$200	On Time	+5	660
5	$4,400	$200	Late by 10 Days	-10	650

⇒Learning Points:

- Late or missed payments can cause major credit score drops.
- On-time payments are one of the biggest positive credit factors.
- Scores can recover with consistency over time.

Credit Mix Scenarios with Score Impact

Scenario	Credit Mix	Behavior	Estimated Impact on Credit Score
1. Thin File Starter	1 Credit Card	Pays on time, 12 months history	Limited impact—small gains
2. Balanced Mix	2 Credit Cards + 1 Car Loan	All accounts in good standing	+15–30 pts over time

3. Poor Mix, High Utilization	3 Credit Cards, No Loans	Utilization over 90%, no payment issues	-10 to -25 pts
4. Added Installment Loan	2 Credit Cards→ Adds Student Loan	Pays on time, diversifies mix	+10–20 pts
5. Early Loan Closure	1 Credit Card + Car Loan (paid off early)	Responsible history, but loan closed too soon	Slight dip (~ -5 pts short-term)
6. Revolving-Only Use	4 Credit Cards, No Loans	Low utilization, never missed a payment	Flat/no gain—weak mix
7. Multiple Types + Late Payment	2 Credit Cards + Car Loan + Student Loan	1 missed student loan payment	-40 pts or more
8. Strong, Seasoned Mix	3 Credit Cards + Mortgage + Auto Loan (10+ yrs)	Long history, no missed payments	+30–50 pts (excellent mix)

⇒Key Takeaways

- Variety matters, but timely payments matter more.
- Adding one loan to a card-only profile can significantly boost your score.
- Too many revolving accounts without loans = stagnant growth.
- A missed payment can erase the benefits of even the best mix.

Types of Debt Overview

Debt Type	Definition	Example	Secured?	Typical Interest
Credit Card	Revolving line of credit with monthly minimums.	Shopping, emergency expenses	No	15–29%
Student Loan	Money borrowed for education, repaid after school ends.	Tuition, books	No (usually)	4–8% (Federal)
Auto Loan	Borrowed money to purchase a car, secured by the vehicle.	Car purchase	Yes	5–13%
Mortgage	Long-term loan to buy a house.	Home loan	Yes	3–8%
Personal Loan	Unsecured loan used for various purposes.	Debt consolidation, emergencies	No	6–36%
Payday Loan	Short-term, high-interest loan due on next payday.	Quick cash fix	No	100–400%
HELOC	Credit line based on equity in your home.	Home remodel	Yes	5–8%

Real-Life Simulation–Debt Repayment Strategies:

Debt	**Balance**	**APR**	**Min Payment**	**Type**
Credit Card A	$500	22%	$25	Credit Card (Unsecured)
Credit Card B	$800	18%	$35	Credit Card (Unsecured)
Personal Loan	$1,500	10%	$75	Personal Loan (Unsecured)

Option A: Snowball Method (smallest balance first)

Month	**Focus**	**Paid Off**	**Motivation Boost**
1–2	Credit Card A		Quick Win
3–4	Credit Card B		Steady Progress
5–12	Personal Loan		Debt-Free!

Option B: Avalanche Method (highest interest first)

Month	**Focus**	**Paid Off**	**Savings Impact**
1–3	Credit Card A		Lower Interest
4–5	Credit Card B		
6–12	Personal Loan		

Section 3: Scenario A–James, Age 32

Situation:

- $15,000 in credit card debt (unsecured), multiple cards
- Living paycheck to paycheck, often over drafting

Plan:

- Build a simple budget
- Call credit card providers for hardship plan
- Use Debt Snowball to gain momentum
- Track expenses and trim subscriptions

Result:

In 24 months, James is debt-free and has a 690+ credit score.

Section 4: Scenario B–Lisa, Age 28

Debts:

Debt Type	Balance	APR
Student Loans (4)	$22,000	5–7%
Credit Cards (2)	$3,000	18–20%
Auto Loan	$10,000	8%

Plan:

- Enroll in income-based repayment on student loans
- Avalanche on credit cards
- Refinance car loan for lower rate
- Budget review and track spending

Result:

Lisa improves her score, avoids car repossession, and creates margin.

Section 5: Budget Cut Challenge

Help participants free $300/month to go toward debt:

Category	Spending	Adjust To	Savings
Entertainment	$250	$100	$150
Subscriptions	$150	$50	$100
Misc. Spending	$200	$150	$50
Total Saved	—	—	$300

Tax Planning & Understanding Your Taxes

Key Tax Concepts and Definitions

Term	Definition
Taxable Income	The portion of income used to calculate how much tax you owe.
Withholding	Taxes taken out of your paycheck by your employer and sent to the IRS.
Filing Status	Defines your tax bracket and standard deduction (e.g. Single, Married).
Standard Deduction	A flat amount that reduces taxable income based on filing status.
Tax Credit	Directly reduces taxes owed (e.g. Child Tax Credit, EITC).
Tax Deduction	Lowers taxable income (e.g. mortgage interest, charitable giving).
Refund	Money returned by the IRS if you overpaid during the year.
Owe/Tax Due	What you must pay the IRS if not enough was withheld throughout the year.

2025 Federal Income Tax Brackets

Rate	Single	Married Filing Jointly	Head of Household
10%	\$0–\$11,600	\$0–\$23,200	\$0–\$16,550
12%	\$11,601–\$47,150	\$23,201–\$94,300	\$16,551–\$63,100
22%	\$47,151–\$100,525	\$94,301–\$201,050	\$63,101–\$100,500
24%	\$100,526–\$191,950	\$201,051–\$383,900	\$100,501–\$191,950
32%	\$191,951–\$243,725	\$383,901–\$487,450	\$191,951–\$243,700
35%	\$243,726–\$609,350	\$487,451–\$731,200	\$243,701–\$609,350
37%	\$609,351+	\$731,201+	\$609,351+

Real-Life Simulation–Tax Withholding Impact

Scenario	W-4 Filing Status	Annual Income	Tax Withheld	Refund/ Owed	Result
Marcus–Single	Single	$42,000	$6,500	Refund: $1,500	Withholding too much. Could increase cash flow by adjusting W-4.
Naomi–Head of Household	Head of Household	$48,000	$3,800	Refund: $4,000	Credits (EITC, CTC) boost refund. Good planning.
Darren–Self-Employed	N/A	$65,000	$0	Owes: $7,000	Missed quarterly payments. Faced penalties. Needs proactive planning.

Real-Life Scenarios

Marcus (Age 29, Single, W-2 Job)

Marcus earns $42,000 annually and didn't adjust his W-4. At tax time, he receives a $1,500 refund. He's happy, but then realizes he could've had an extra $125/month throughout the year by adjusting his W-4 to more accurately reflect his tax burden.

Lesson: Many people overpay into taxes during the year. Adjusting your withholding can give you more usable income monthly.

Darren (Age 46, Self-Employed Handyman)

Darren makes $65,000 but doesn't pay quarterly taxes throughout the year. He ends up owing over $7,000 in income tax and self-employment tax, plus penalties. This leads to unexpected financial stress.

Lesson: Self-employed people must plan for taxes by making quarterly payments and setting aside money throughout the year.

2025 Tax Updates for Middle-Income Earners (With Changes from 2024)

Update	2024 Amount	2025 Amount	Change	What It Means for You
Standard Deduction (Single)	$13,850	$14,600	+ $750	Lowers taxable income more than last year.
Standard Deduction (Married Filing Jointly)	$27,700	$29,200	+ $1,500	Helps couples keep more of their income.
Standard Deduction (Head of Household)	$20,800	$21,900	+ $1,100	Greater benefit for single parents or caregivers.
Earned Income Credit (w/ 1 child)	~$4,000	~$4,200	+ ~$200	More refund potential for working families.
401(k) Contribution Limit	$23,000 *(incl. catch-up)*	$23,500 *(projected)*	+ $500 *(est.)*	Save more pre-tax for retirement.
IRA Contribution Limit (under 50)	$7,000	$7,500 *(projected)*	+ $500 *(est.)*	Higher savings potential, especially if not covered by a workplace plan.
Child Tax Credit	$2,000 per child	$2,200	+200	Still available to help families with qualifying children.

Understanding Life Insurance: Protection First, Then Wealth

1. Why Life Insurance?

Main purpose: Protect your family if you die.

Life insurance can replace your income and help pay debts, mortgage, kids' expenses, and final costs.

Key question: "If I died today, who would struggle financially tomorrow?"

2. Main Types of Life Insurance

A. Term Life–"Temporary Income Protection"

- Covers you for a set time (10, 20, 30 years)
- Pays a lump sum (death benefit) if you die during that term
- No savings or investment–pure protection
- Usually the cheapest way to get a lot of coverage
- Best for families with kids, people with a mortgage/debts, and anyone needing protection while others depend on their income

B. Whole Life–"Lifetime Coverage + Cash Value"

- Coverage for your entire life (as long as you pay)
- Builds cash value you can borrow against
- Premiums are much higher than term for the same coverage
- Used for lifetime coverage (burial, inheritance) and long-term planning when income is strong

C. Universal / Indexed / Variable Life–"Flexible & Complex"

- Permanent coverage with flexible premiums and cash value
- Cash value growth may be tied to interest, a market index, or investments
- More moving parts and more risk if not funded well
- Usually for advanced planning with a professional

3. Can Life Insurance Be a Wealth Tool?

Cash-value policies (Whole, UL, IUL, VUL) can:

- Grow cash value over time (often with tax advantages)
- Be borrowed against
- Provide a tax-free death benefit under current rules But they:
- Cost more than term
- Often grow slower than retirement accounts (401(k), IRA, Roth, etc.)
- Can lose value if canceled early

Healthy order:

1. Protection first–get enough coverage so your family is safe
2. Basic wealth tools–emergency fund, pay high-interest debt, save for retirement
3. Advanced tools (cash-value insurance)–maybe later, once basics are solid

4. What Insurance Do I Need?

If you have a spouse, kids, or others depending on your income:

- Common starting point: 10–15× your annual income in coverage
- Make sure it can help cover income replacement, mortgage/major debts, childcare/kids' education, and final expenses

If you're single with no dependents:

- You may only need basic coverage for debts and funeral costs
- Term life is usually very cheap when you're young and healthy

5. How Do I Decide Which Policy to Buy?

1. Who am I protecting? (Spouse, kids, parents, or others relying on my income)
2. How much coverage do I need? (Rough rule: 10–15× annual income + big debts + final expenses)
3. What type fits my situation? (Most people: level term life, 20–30 years, for affordable protection)
4. Compare companies and options (premium cost, company financial strength, convertibility, riders)

6. Key Takeaways

- Life insurance is first a protection tool, not a get-rich-quick plan
- For most people, the priority is affordable term life with enough coverage

- Cash-value insurance can play a role in wealth-building, but usually after you are properly insured, have an emergency fund, and are consistently investing for retirement

Will vs. Trust

Big Idea: A will is mainly about what happens after you die. A revocable living trust can manage your money while you are alive, if you become disabled, and after you die – with more control, but more cost and setup.

1. Basic Definitions

Will

- A legal document that says who gets your property after you die and who is in charge of your estate.
- Only takes effect at death and usually must go through probate court.

Revocable Living Trust

- A legal arrangement where you place assets into a trust you control during your life.
- Names a successor trustee to manage assets if you become incapacitated and after you die.
- Can be changed or revoked while you are alive and competent.

2. Pros and Cons at a Glance

	Will	Revocable Living Trust
Cost to set up	Lower upfront cost, usually simpler	Higher upfront cost (attorney time and paperwork)
Probate	Usually must go through probate (public, can be slow and add costs)	Can avoid probate for assets properly titled in the trust
Incapacity planning	Does not help if you are alive but incapacitated – you need separate powers of attorney	Successor trustee can step in and manage trust assets without going to court
Privacy	Probate is often public; will may become part of the public record	Generally private – terms of trust and asset list are not public
Control over distributions	Simpler, often lump-sum gifts or basic instructions	More control: staggered distributions, conditions, long-term management for kids or vulnerable beneficiaries
Complexity & upkeep	Easier to understand; minimal ongoing maintenance	More moving parts; must "fund" the trust by retitling assets and reviewing over time

3. When a Will May Be Enough

- You have a relatively simple situation: one home, basic accounts, and straightforward heirs.
- You are comfortable with your estate going through probate in your state.
- Your main goals are to name who gets what and to appoint guardians for minor children.

4. When a Trust Is Often Better

- You want to make things easier and more private for your family by avoiding probate.
- You own multiple properties, a business, or assets in more than one state.
- You have minor children, a child with special needs, or beneficiaries who need help managing money.
- You care about clear management of your assets if you become disabled or incapacitated.

5. Key Myths to Clarify

- "Trusts are only for the rich" – Many middle-class families use trusts mainly to avoid probate and simplify things.
- "A trust replaces the need for a will" – Most people with a trust still use a simple "pour-over" will and need powers of attorney.
- "A trust eliminates all taxes" – A basic revocable living trust usually does not reduce income or estate taxes on its own.

www.ingramcontent.com/pod-product-compliance
Lightning Source LLC
LaVergne TN
LVHW010703110826
845149LV00014B/3219

* 9 7 9 8 9 9 1 5 3 9 5 7 9 *